PHYLLIS:
LOVE NEVER LETS GO

- - A MEMOIR - -

BOB JONES

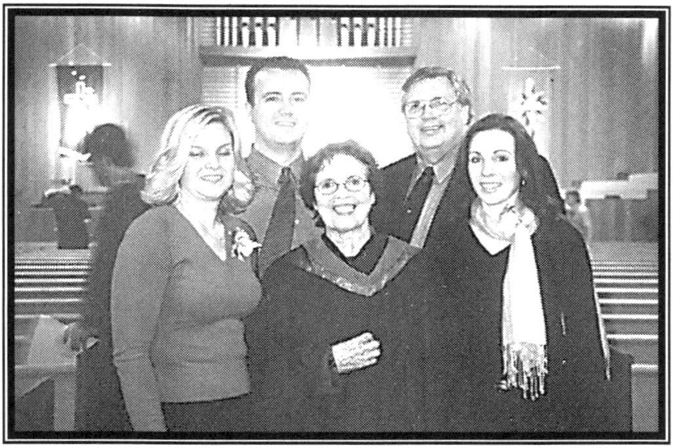

CONTENTS

i.	Writing this memoire	1
ii.	Introduction	7
1	Abandoned	11
2	Refuge In Coby	17
3	God's Love Never Let's Go	19
4	Training For Ministry	23
5	A Man Named Bruce	27
6	Renal Failure	33
7	Dialysis	35
8	God Answers Prayer	39
9	Transplant	41
10	Pastoring – Part 1	45

11	Parenting	53
12	Pastoring – Part 2	57
13	Chaplaincy	63
14	A Second Kidney Donor	71
15	Caroline, Karen & Phyllis	75
16	The Big Talk	85
17	When You Can't Comeback	91
18	An Appointment With God	95
19	Slipping The Bonds Of Earth	99
20	See You In The Morning	103
21	Lessons For My Grandchildren	107

APPENDIX	115
ACKNOWLEDGEMENTS	149
ABOUT THE AUTHOR	149

WRITING THIS MEMOIR

When Phyllis Fisher asked, "Bob, will you help me write my story?" there was only one possible reply.

My "yes" was out there before I fully thought through what I was committing to.

But how could I say no?

Besides the fact that I owed Bruce and Phyllis Fisher a debt of gratitude, it was nigh unto impossible to say "no" to Phyllis.

My future became intertwined with the Fishers long before Bruce tied the knot between my wife, Jocelyn and I on May 19, 1979.

Eastern Pentecostal Bible College (EPBC) in Peterborough, Ontario was where Jocelyn Blades and I met. She was there because Bruce and Phyllis had enough confidence in her as a nineteen year old to appoint her as their youth leader at Bethany

Church in Saint John, NB. They saw great potential and God's calling in her young life and Bible College became her next step.

Jocelyn was inspired by Phyllis to believe she could be used in ministry and was supported by her in 1976 when she headed off halfway across Canada to go to EPBC.

Years later our families were called to neighboring churches in Montreal, Quebec. Phyllis became a mentor to Jocelyn as a pastor's wife and a mom with two pre-school sons.

In 1990 Bruce invited me to join his staff as he transitioned to Central Tabernacle in Edmonton, Alberta. Along with Bruce, Emmanuel Fonte and Steve Hertzog we became known at Central as the "wise men from the East." Phyllis "mothered" her boys without smothering us with hospitality and support.

In those days the senior pastor's wife traditionally served as the "President" of the women's ministry. Phyllis invited Jocelyn to fill that role on her behalf. Then she became Jocelyn's loyal supporter.

When Bruce's failing health necessitated taking a part-time leadership role, he appointed me his Associate. Later he went on full disability and I became the interim pastor in his place.

In May 1994 our lives went full circle when Jocelyn and I were asked to become the lead pastor at Central and we became Phyllis and Bruce's pastors. The significance of this rare relationship was never lost on us. Phyllis was Jocelyn's biggest cheerleader. Jocelyn reflected on those days, "She inspired me to believe I could be the senior pastor's wife of a significant kingdom church."

Being asked to work with Phyllis in creating a legacy piece for her grandchildren was a privilege. The afternoons we spent together recording her memories were sacred times. Often, her granddaughters would arrive at the Fisher condo as I was leaving from our interviews and I could see first hand the love they shared.

Our writing journey began in her living room on March 9, 2017. We met for a second interview on March 17th - Saint Patrick's Day. A fitting time as Phyllis was proud of her Irish heritage. There was no blarney in her answer when I asked how she was feeling. "I'm at a five out of ten on a pain scale. Three would be a threshold where some attention needs to be paid to my pain level. But that's OK."

On March 23rd I was introduced to a friend of Phyllis' and the woman who donated one of her kidneys to Phyllis in 2006. I listened in on a lively conversation. None of us had any idea that two months later to the day Phyllis would be in heaven.

We met again on March 31st, April 5th and April 18th. Ministry commitments took me out of town for the next three weeks. I fully expected to see her in the 2nd week of May. Sadly, by then, she was in tertiary care. Our conversations came to an end.

What impressed me in story after story was Phyllis's desire to please the Lord and share what she felt was from the Lord. Though tending to prefer background roles in ministry – especially on Sundays - Phyllis could be quite bold when she felt the moving of the Holy Spirit. She was known for giving public expressions during church services – a word of prophecy, or exhortation. She felt an empowerment that helped her do what she did.

Though she was born into a broken family, she instinctively knew how to make her family work.

Phyllis never used her illness or pain to deflect her drive to care for people and it was easy for those looking on to think she never had a care in the world beyond those they knew about.

Phyllis underwent two kidney transplants. Her desire was for people to be assured that organ transplants work. She conferred with many patients who were afraid to have a transplant and when she told them how long she had her transplant they'd respond, "You have been how long?" When she reached thirty years as a transplant patient, her story was about encouraging other people, not about her.

Phyllis was effervescent, genuinely loved and accepted people as they were. She didn't have a judgmental bone in her body. Making other people feel recognized and important was Phyllis' mission. She excelled at it.

When Rev. Billy Graham passed away in February 2018, his personal spokesperson and media representative, for over thirty years, A. Larry Ross said, "Mr. Graham was able to connect with anyone — especially airport porters, hotel maids or restaurant waitpersons - and made anyone in his presence feel important."

Ditto that for Rev. Phyllis Fisher. Phyllis made anyone she encountered feel significant. Modesty, humility and sincerity were the hallmarks of her character.

Perhaps you are one of those on whom she impressed the confidence to achieve a fruitful life and ministry.

That was my experience with her.

And I am grateful I said "yes".

Bob Jones
Lead Pastor, North Pointe Community Church, 2018

INTRODUCTION

"Gone to get a kidney. Love, Phyllis"

That was so Phyllis.

Concise. Caring. Sunny.

The hurried note left on the table for her new husband Bruce was a matter-of-fact reminder of how Phyllis approached life.

Minutes earlier she received a phone call from her attending physician. It was the call she had long anticipated and prayed for.

"You need to get to the hospital right away."

"I can't."

"What do you mean you can't?"

"I've got to take a bus because there is no one to drive me."

Her doctor pointedly told her, "No. Take a taxi."

"I don't have any money to pay for a taxi."

She could feel the urgency in her doctor's voice as he told her to call a taxi and he would pay for it.

"Get here. Now."

On the way to the hospital Phyllis could hardly contain her joy. She eagerly informed the taxi driver, "I'm going to get a kidney." No response. As though he didn't just hear the best news in the entire universe.

What can you do when you have no one to share your excitement with? She thought she'd explode but better not because her dream was so close to coming true.

"Bruce will be so happy."

When she arrived at the hospital, attendants were impatiently waiting for her. As she got out of the taxi they scolded, "Where have you been?"

Phyllis explained, "Well, I had to pack my suitcase."

As she lay on the gurney waiting for the donor kidney Phyllis was sobered by the thought that someone else died in order for her to be the recipient of this kidney.

"I'm no one special, Lord. Why me?"

Never in her wildest dreams would she have envisioned the special purpose that God had for that donated organ. Even further from her imagination was the fact she would have not one, but two kidney transplants in her lifetime, and become one of the longest surviving transplant patients in Canadian history.

How could she have known this kidney would change the future for her and literally thousands of people who would be influenced by Rev. Phyllis Ryan Fisher.

People like me.

The effects of her life are forever rippling out in ever expanding circles of love. If you haven't yet felt their influence you soon will.

This memoir is carried on those ripples.

CHAPTER 1
Abandoned

Phyllis Ryan was born on December 19th, 1947 in York, Toronto.

Mom and dad Ryan separated around the time Phyllis was two. The fallout forever scarred her. She filtered everything in life through the heartbreaking effects of abandonment. Even as a wife and mother in healthy relationships she felt the icy grip of mistrust and anxiety.

Over the following fifteen years, upheaval would characterize Phyllis' existence. Her mother was employed in an arsenal, a part of the war experience. However, soon after the war ended she was laid off. Work became very difficult to find, especially for a woman. As time went on she had less and less income, which would require more moves to smaller and smaller apartments.

"What doesn't kill you makes you stronger" played out as truth for Phyllis. From a young age her ever-changing circumstances bred a strong sense of self and independence. Soon she was travelling alone - at the age of five. Her mother would put her on a bus in Lindsay, Ontario and she would travel over two hours to Toronto to meet her extended family.

As an elementary student she was trusted to purchase her own clothes with her mom's money – and her mom's preferences. Her sense of style got the better of her once when she purchased colored shoes rather than the saddle shoes her mother preferred because the colored shoes were much more attractive.

In grades 1, 2 and 3 the girls at Phyllis' school here expected to wear a uniform - navy blue tunic, white blouse, blue socks and black shoes. She wore the same tunic from Grade 1 to Grade 3. Her school photos tell the awkward tale because her tunic looked shorter with each passing year. Phyllis' expression in her class photos made her stand out from all the other students. She was as cute as a button with million-dollar smile.

Grade 9 class photos reveal a shift in Phyllis' perspective. No longer is she smiling because she had become self-conscious – she thought her smile was too big.

Phyllis found herself getting deeply frustrated and angry over the frequent moves related to her mom's work situation. Their mother/daughter time was drastically curtailed by the time she was in Grade 5. Her mom's life was occupied looking after the children of a widower. Whether it was from jealousy or neglect, Phyllis started drifting into bad habits. She was smoking when she was only ten years old. In her words Phyllis was growing into "a real hellion" - jumping out of barn doors into hay bales with a cigarette in her mouth.

She soon became too much for her mom to handle. Fiercely proud and independent, her mom was humbled by being forced to ask friends, the Endicott family, if Phyllis could board with them. Phyllis would never again live with her mom.

The Endicotts lived on an acreage and had five daughters. In some ways Phyllis became daughter #6. Thelma Endicott became like a mom to her. You could imagine Phyllis' family experience if you are familiar with the story of "Little Women." Even their horse was female. Phyllis remembers it as a wonderful life and gave her insight into how to live with others in a family situation. Even though she had to ask permission to go to the fridge, she felt at least like she mattered.

The Omemee area public school, just outside of Peterborough, was where Phyllis received her elementary education. Entering Grade 9 meant that she would need to attend Fenelon Falls High School. That meant leaving the Endicotts, which was devastating for Phyllis. She would now have to move in with other friends of her mother - the Pogue family.

By the time Phyllis turned thirteen she had moved thirteen times.

As a child she had had no memory of her father. She was informed that her father had two brothers and three sisters. One of those sisters lived in Toronto. Phyllis was sent to visit her on weekends. It was on one of those weekend visits that she recalls travelling with her aunt in a car. Her aunt pointed to a large, stately home - "This is where your grandmother lives." As they passed the home Phyllis instinctively knew that was turf she wouldn't be able to venture on.

She was told that her father attended a parochial school when he was an adolescent. Yes, he was studying to be a Catholic priest. His sacred career was cut short when was caught in the wine cellar and kicked out of school. As an adult he was employed in food delivery, travelling between Montreal and British Columbia. Solo travel suited him because he was a loner by preference.

In grade ten, Phyllis learned that her mom was applying for a divorce from her dad. Her father was not interested in remarrying or divorcing. Because her mother could not afford the lawyer fees to proceed, the divorce never went through.

Phyllis longed to find her dad. She didn't want to hurt her mom by her looking for her dad so she asked God to help her find her father. She felt prompted to write to her mother's lawyer and asked him to send her any addresses that he had for her father. The last address the lawyer had was from Vancouver, BC. So she wrote her dad a letter and sent him her grade ten class photo. She remembers very distinctly that she was wearing her favorite blue-colored sweater in the photo.

Her father's last address was a boarding house on Melville Street in Vancouver. He had not lived at that boarding house for over two years. He was living in Dawson Creek, BC employed as a hotel receptionist. As God would have it, he showed up at the Vancouver boarding house three weeks after the letter arrived.

Both Phyllis and her father recognized the coincidental timing as a miracle of God. The experience became a cornerstone for Phyllis in knowing that God does answer prayer and works miracles.

Mr. Ryan was a wonderful writer and sent Phyllis a most beautiful letter in reply. He assured Phyllis that her mother was not responsible for the break up of the family. He wrote to her, "I was always loved but I did not know how to love in return." That phrase had a real impact on Phyllis. She says that those are some of the loneliest words that a person could say.

Included in the letter was his Alcoholics Anonymous membership card, which had on it the twelve steps of the recovery program. That card explained so much of the addictive influence her father fought and contributed to the breakup of their family.

He also included his phone number. A clear invitation for connection and Phyllis was thrilled to call him right away. His mother had died just a few days before Phyllis called. She became his comforter. In that first call she learned she had twenty-three cousins on her father's side that she had never met.

They renewed their relationship through correspondence. He would often correct her letters, marking them in red and then sending them back to her. Phyllis jokingly says her father had a "very perfectionist nature."

Her father helped Phyllis believe that coming from a broken home doesn't mean you can't have a family of your own in the future. He inspired her to want to have her own family.

CHAPTER 2
Refuge In Coby

One April afternoon in 2017 I asked Phyllis, "If you could have one wish to create a new memory what would it be?" Immediately she replied, "A special day in the mountains with my family." Since moving out West, she'd developed a fondness for Canmore, Maligne Lake and Jasper, Alberta. The grandeur of the mountains and access to wildlife enthralled her.

Then, very quickly, she changed her answer. "I would love to take my grandchildren and spend a day by a freshwater lake in Ontario, especially in the Kawarthas, so they could see what was a part of my childhood and the beauty that I was surrounded by."

That's when I learned about "Coby."

The village of Coboconk lies at the junction of Highway 35 and former Highway 48, on the northern tip of Balsam Lake. For Phyllis, Coboconk – or "Coby" as she affectionately called the village – became her refuge in life.

Her aunt Maisie owned and ran a small but popular restaurant called the "Kawartha Tea Room." As a child, most of Phyllis' travels were from the town of Lindsay to Coby. She loved being with her aunt Maisie. Her living quarters were in the restaurant. How cool – to live in a restaurant. Phyllis began working at the restaurant at age 12 during holidays and on weekends.

Phyllis got to know everyone in the little village, including Percy. Percy was a senior suffering from mental illness. He was very particular about who took his order – which was typically a Sweet Marie chocolate bar and a Coke. When he came to the Tea Room he insisted only Aunt Maisie could take his money. He trusted her. Over time Percy began to soften up to Phyllis. What a proud day it was when he told her that he trusted Phyllis. "You could take my money."

Because of Maisie, Coby felt like the closest thing to a hometown for Phyllis. And family. Though she was cared for by the Endicotts and the Pogues, aunt Maisie was her only blood relative that made her feel cherished.

No matter where she lived for the rest of her life, Phyllis always needed assurance that she would have access to going back to Coby and aunt Maisie.

Later in her senior years, as her health declined and she sold the restaurant, Maisie was invited by Phyllis to come and live with her. Until Maisie's death, Phyllis insured that she would never be alone.

CHAPTER 3
God's Love Never Lets Go

In the 50's there weren't a lot of broken homes. Growing up without her parents left Phyllis feeling very much alone, isolated, and vulnerable. These circumstances became the ready soil for the seeds of love of God.

Phyllis' mother wasn't a churchgoer and her father described himself as a lapsed Catholic. Even without the influence of a church, the Spirit of God has a way of getting through to children. When she was eight or nine she was given a Bible. Simply by reading parts of the New Testament Phyllis learned about Jesus.

He loved little girls like her.

And he died on the cross for her sins.

One evening, alone in her room, Phyllis began to weep. Getting down on her knees by her bed, she asked God to forgive her sins. No one explained faith or repentance or salvation to her, but she understood. Phyllis later attributed her experience to the sovereign workings of the Holy Spirit. In her tender heart she had felt so afraid that God would reject her because of her family situation.

God's love began to heal many of her wounds.

In trying to explain her encounter with God, the story of Samuel comes to mind as illustrative of what Phyllis experienced. Samuel was a little boy who heard God's audible voice and understood and responded. Phyllis was a little girl who heard God's voice through reading the Bible and responded to Him.

She had a very special relationship with God - as though she was God's child from the beginning. She had little to do with her salvation. All on her own she became a dedicated child of God.

The Endicott family with whom she boarded, attended a United church in the country. The tiny building was usually packed with parishioners. They attended in the afternoon so chores could be done. Phyllis' quest for God began in that church. An aunt of the Endicott girls was the Sunday school teacher and said that if they learn nothing else from the Bible to understand the content of John 3:16. That touched Phyllis' heart deeply. She was 11.

Hearing that Jesus loved her just as she was, was affirming and welcome. She was overwhelmed by the love of God. She became very passionate about her faith. And influential. She shared with anyone who would listen to her talk about Jesus.

Years later, Barb Endicott called Phyllis to tell her she had just come to her personal faith in Jesus. On Easter Sunday 2017 Barb called again to remind Phyllis of how much her talking about Jesus with "the little women's group" made a huge difference in their lives. The conversation was like a "thank you" note from God. Phyllis felt pleased knowing that she had some small influence on Barb's life.

The second family she boarded with – the Pogues - also was a family of faith. They attended the Pentecostal church in Bobcaygeon. It was through the Pentecostal church that Phyllis was assured she did not need religious rituals to be accepted by God. In the United Church she required "confirmation" in order to be accepted. She was not allowed to take communion. In some ways going to church elicited a lonely feeling - rejection. She knew no one else who came from a broken home.

The Pentecostals accepted her as she was. The Pentecostal church didn't have a great reputation in the community. No one wanted to hang with the "holy rollers" or "chandelier swingers." She didn't care. Phyllis was accepted and that's where she decided to follow Jesus.

It was there she learned about the Baptism in the Holy Spirit and observed what outsiders considered "strange" – speaking in tongues, words of prophecy, and people falling down under the power of the Holy Spirit. Rather than feel tentative she was intrigued. On December 10, 1961 Phyllis was baptized in the Holy Spirit on a Sunday night at the church. Rev. Art Ettinger was the pastor. He prayed for her and she began to speak in tongues as the Holy Spirit gave her the words.

As much as being filled with the Holy Spirit was powerful, her salvation was so significant to her that the baptism in the Holy

Spirit, though important, didn't radically change her spiritual life.

A lot of her friends were not into church when she was growing up. She was teased for her faith but she was undeterred. Phyllis was very happy to have friends who were not churchgoers and she knew she was called to be salt and light for them.

One of her biggest teasers later became a friend and a fellow believer.

CHAPTER 4
Training for Ministry

Phyllis was sixteen years old when she felt the call to ministry. It happened during a Sunday evening church service. "There were no audible words but I knew that God spoke to me. Somehow He wanted to use my life in ministry. My impression was it would be in chaplaincy."

Her mother was quite unenthused with her inclination to go to Bible College to train for ministry, much less marry a pastor.

Students in Ontario who felt called to ministry went to Bible College. And Eastern Pentecostal Bible College in Peterborough was the only college familiar to Phyllis. A year later she applied. Part of the application process entailed a pastor's recommendation. She asked her pastor, Rev. Art Ettinger, if he would write a recommendation for her.

Pastor Ettinger would not give her a good reference. He called her aside and talked to her about her church attendance and her make up. Both had to change.

She wore lipstick and a bit of eyebrow pencil, which were no-no's for good Pentecostal girls, especially ones aspiring to ministry.

Regular attendance at Sunday night church services was a second failing. Sunday was a social day. Following a Sunday morning church service was time to be with friends from high school. Afternoon activities would turn into dinner at a friend's house and before she knew it, she'd missed the evening service. While Phyllis went to church always on Sunday mornings and some Sunday nights, her pastor was quite strict and expected everybody to show up for every service. If you didn't show up you weren't quite recommendable for Bible College.

So, Phyllis showed up every Sunday night and got rid of the make up. She thought about the fact that nuns have to give up family life and adopt a strict lifestyle and she had to give up lipstick. No big deal to Phyllis. However, she had recently died her hair raven black and now she had no lipstick. So her appearance was very stark.

Hardly anybody noticed that she had even worn make up. When Phyllis threw away her lipstick and make-up - which was expensive - Max Factor and Cover Girl - the young ladies in the home where she was staying retrieved them from the garbage for their own personal use.

Strangely enough, the initial reference for Phyllis to Bible College from Pastor Ettinger never got through to the Administration.

In the meantime Phyllis had "pulled up her socks" and Pastor

Art was able to write a new reference. The second one was far more favorable for Phyllis. She was over the moon when her acceptance letter arrived.

Bible College played a significant role in Phyllis' life because for the first time she was surrounded by peers who were interested in studying the Bible and pursuing ministry just like she was.

Eastern Pentecostal Bible College rules were very strict by today's standards. No earrings, no make up, no slacks except on Thursdays when they could go skating. After skating Phyllis and her friends would skip dinner so they could wear their slacks into the evening in their rooms.

In the fall during commencement, students were expected to help clean up the campus. The girls would wear slacks to do the landscaping, outdoor work, cleaning windows and the like. Representatives from the District Office touring the campus saw them in their slacks and spoke to the Bible College leaders and insisted they should not be allowed to wear them in public. The next year they were required to wear dresses to do yard work. Phyllis wisely didn't allow those "small potato kind of things" to deter her from pursuing learning about the call to ministry and everything that goes on that's truly important at a Bible College.

Phyllis had a roommate in Bible College who had a background similar to hers. Faye came from Shawville in the Ottawa Valley. She was like Phyllis in the sense that they both knew what it was like to live and work and be with people who didn't go to church. It seemed like many of the other students had grown up in environment where everyone they knew went to church or were

Christians. So the other students were appalled when Phyllis and Faye would wash their hair on a Sunday night, which was another Pentecostal no-no.

Faye and Phyllis shared the same crazy sense of humor. They loved a good laugh. Her sense of humor made a good impression on Phyllis' family. They roomed all three years together and when Phyllis got married she asked Faye to be her maid of honor.

CHAPTER 5
A Man Named Bruce

Bible College isn't affectionately known as "bridal college" for nothing.

It wasn't long before Phyllis caught the eye of a very eligible bachelor student named Bruce Fisher. Bruce was tall, dark, handsome, somewhat reserved and very serious. When they first met, Bruce informed her he didn't want to date just to date.

Following their first date, Bruce wrote Phyllis a letter. "If we started to date would you take that seriously?" Here was a man who meant business. He was devoted in his calling to ministry and had no time or margin to get side-tracked by someone who was less serious than he was. He closed his letter with, "After you read this you must destroy the letter." Being respectful and somewhat smitten, Phyllis obliged.

Oh how she wished she could have that letter back for posterity.

Phyllis had few positive male figures in her life.

Her father abandoned her.
Her uncle was ill.
Her mom remarried to a man who was unambitious.
She lived with the Endicott family who had five daughters and the Pogue family who had two girls.
Phyllis grew up with an all-female influence.

Then along came Bruce. His masculinity impressed her.

He was a responsible man - the first she knew. He was decisive, confident, assured and trustworthy. She liked that. Just trusting men was hard for her. It was very important that she respect Bruce because she had to trust him.

Their fellow Bible college classmates noticed that Phyllis started taking piano lessons. This was somewhat puzzling as she had never evidenced an inclination to be a musician. Phyllis enjoyed music but God did not bless her with musical talent. Why the piano, now?

The logic of love. Bruce had a beautiful baritone voice. Students, especially the female ones, felt he would marry a musician. So Phyllis took piano lessons because everyone knew that "all good wives of pastors play the piano."

And when she was teased by some of students she gave up out of embarrassment.

Later in life, a pastor's wife who was very musical told Phyllis, "I would do anything to get off this piano and go around and pray for people like you." That was an eye-opener for Phyllis because she felt that she was inferior because she didn't have any musical ability.

Bruce says, "She didn't have to be a musician to be a minister. She was a wonderful blessing just as she was. A better blessing, because I could find other gifted musicians but not such a wonderful wife."

Bruce asked Phyllis' mom for permission to marry Phyllis. Her mother was concerned. She feared Phyllis would end up as a pastor's wife not really having much in life like other women with men who pursued more lucrative careers.

When Phyllis became deathly ill, Bruce was so devoted to her care, her mother's opinion of Bruce completely changed. Bruce's commitment to Phyllis and his follow through with getting married influenced her family in a good way more than anything else.

He could do no wrong.

30

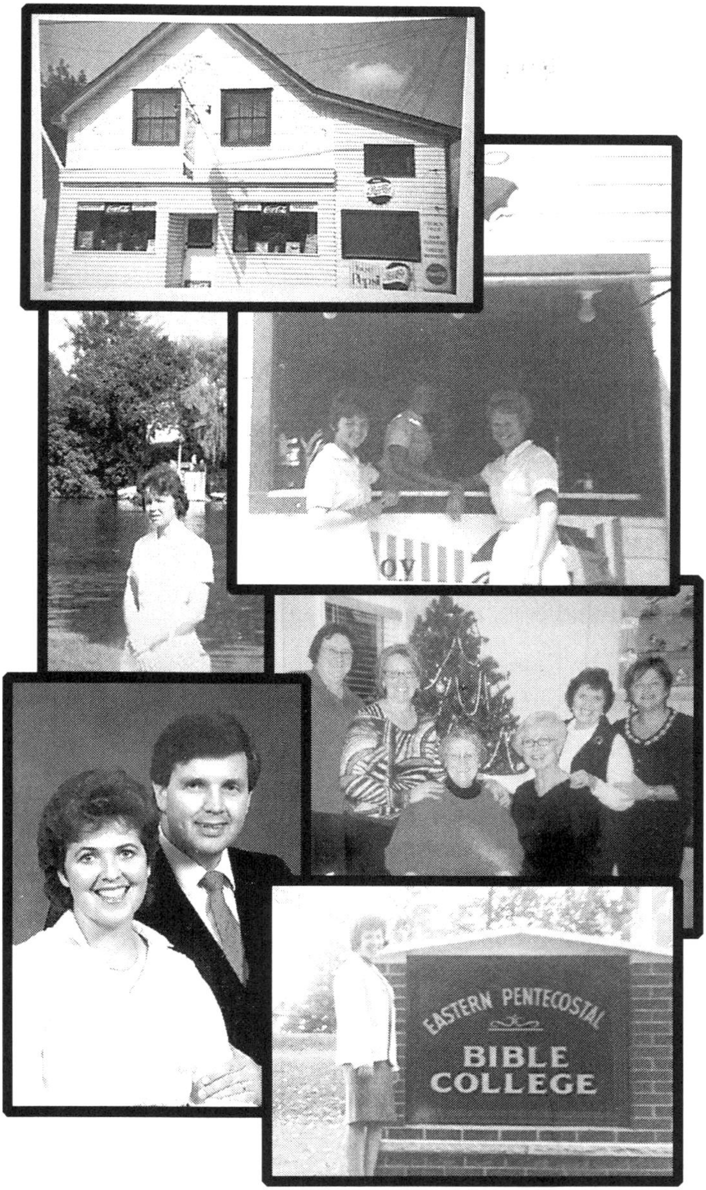
EASTERN PENTECOSTAL
BIBLE
COLLEGE

CHAPTER 6
Renal Failure

Bruce and Phyllis were engaged in 1968 just after graduating Bible College. In July 1968 Phyllis was boarding with a girlfriend in a basement apartment in Scarborough and working in downtown Toronto at the Loblaws head office. Bruce was working on the Gaspé coast. It was a Friday afternoon. Phyllis had been feeling unwell and booked an appointment to go see her GP on the following Monday. Her boss took one look at her and said, "Go today." Had she delayed until Monday she would have been dead.

"I was very fortunate my doctor happened to be at Toronto Western Hospital. So I called him and went to his office. I had to go all the way back via buses to Scarborough. When I got to Scarborough I was running out of breath." Doctors ran tests on her. They discovered her kidneys were failing.

Phyllis couldn't get in touch with Bruce to let him know what was happening. They had planned to meet that weekend in Toronto at the train station and then travel to aunt Maisie's in

Coby.

Unknown to Phyllis, Bruce had planned to arrive early to surprise her and happened to get to Toronto on the very night that she went into hospital. Her friend met Bruce at the train station around ten o'clock and he used his clergy ID to get into the hospital. Phyllis was diagnosed with anemia, heart failure and her blood pressure was high enough to be at stroke level. She went on 24-hour urine collection and a creatine poison count.

By Saturday they knew that she was in complete renal failure.

A cleansing process of peritoneal dialysis was prescribed to rid her body of poison. A thin tube called a canula was inserted into Phyllis' stomach. The tube was hooked onto an IV pole. Her lifeline.

Not far down the hall she heard a man screaming and dying at the same time.

CHAPTER 7
Dialysis

In the 60's, patients on renal dialysis were hooked up to a machine that "looked like your grandmother's old wash tub." At that time, because so much blood would leave the body, an infusion of blood was needed. That's one of the biggest differences between dialysis then and dialysis now. In the 60's, patients had peritoneal dialysis. Physicians would go in through Phyllis' stomach - frozen with three needles - and then make an incision and she would push up with her stomach and they would push down with the canula.

It was a very crude procedure. Through a process of osmosis the meds went into the stomach through the canula, and drew out the poisons into another receptacle. The process was indescribably painful. During one dialysis procedure in 1968 she had twenty-one needles and seven punctures. The fluids were going in but they weren't coming out. In telling the story Phyllis compared herself to "a fountain in the park." Her ninety-five pound body had numerous puncture wounds in it from previous procedures and they were oozing medication and fluid.

"It was the night I wanted to die."

To distract herself from the pain she imagined what it would be like to die and how she could prepare for death. "If I just fold my arms across my chest I'll be ready to die." Forty-nine years after the experience she remarks how funny that sounds but back then it was very serious.

"I knew that I was not the one to call the shots on my living or my dying. The pain continued and they had given up trying to dialyze this way. It was actually a blessing in disguise because I got on new dialysis treatment quicker."

A tube was inserted on the arterial side of her arm and went back out on the other side. It looked like a horseshoe. If the tube hooked up to the artery slipped off during the procedure patients could bleed to death. She had to wear what she called "dog teeth" - two dogtooth clamps that she wore around her neck that would be used to clamp off the tube in her arm if it became dislodged.

A new kind of treatment made use of "horse serum" as an anti-rejection drug. White blood cells from a human were transplanted into a horse and the horse created anti-bodies. The anti-bodies were transplanted into the renal patients.

As the serum was put into her body it was combined with a saline solution and was so painful that "you cried the whole time it was being used. It felt like fire."

The medication was like two tides coming together in the vein. "You had a woman at the end of the bed telling you to cough at the same time as you had this thing going into your veins. And you had somebody else drying blood on the other arm. You're not thinking warm fuzzy Christian thoughts at that time. "

During one dialysis Phyllis' shunt was leaking and attendants wanted to x-ray the place. In order to do that a dye was injected into her. While she was waiting, she could hear another woman, whom she thought was having the same process. She could hear screams coming out of the woman's room that were so intense it sounded like an animal. And Phyllis remembers thinking, "I think I will go. I'm not going to go through that."

In fear and trembling she walked into the procedure room. Her arm was strapped to the bed and fortunately the dye was going the same direction as the artery.

All through July, August and September, Phyllis endured the dialysis process. Her October wedding date was fast approaching but not as quickly as she was losing weight. Her weight was dropping so fast she had to keep getting her wedding dress refitted. She was down to ninety-five pounds the week before her wedding.

The specialists were very candid with Bruce so he would know exactly what he was getting into by marrying Phyllis. They sincerely advised Bruce that if he was going into ministry that he should not marry Phyllis because she could not take the stress of ministry. She would never be able to have children or have a normal family life together.

Bruce's response was that he loved Phyllis and he looked at marriage as a very serious commitment – one that you do not walk away from it at the first sign of difficulty. The doctors allowed them to get married on the condition that they would not have a wedding ceremony with guests in attendance or a meal to be served. Phyllis did not have the energy or capacity for a crowd. They had to say "no" to traditional things that occurred during a wedding and a reception. There was concern that the ceremony might have to be cancelled at the last minute.

On Thanksgiving weekend she was released from the hospital on Friday night after dialysis. She went from the hospital to home, slept some and then off to church. They were married on an October Saturday afternoon in a little church in Bobcaygeon.

CHAPTER 8
God Answers Prayer

Prayer went hand-in-hand with dialysis.

Phyllis believed God could heal her and she was open to whatever means He may use. At the invitation of a friend, she went back to Eastern Pentecostal Bible College in Peterborough for a series of prayer meetings. Rev. Graham Noble, a highly respected pastor from Newfoundland was the speaker. Her friends shared so admiringly about him that it created a hunger for Phyllis to hear what he had to say. She skipped a session of dialysis to attend. A room was provided at the College along with the care of a teacher, Carol Dudgeon.

In the last service of the week, Phyllis responded to an invitation from Pastor Noble for prayer. He didn't know her or her needs. He simply placed his hands on her head and interceded for her. At the end of the prayer he specifically told her, "Do not pay attention to the signs around you but to the faithfulness of God."

Before Phyllis attended the special meetings, the doctors posted her potassium levels and poison levels on a chalkboard in her hospital room. The levels showed that nothing had changed in Phyllis' body from the treatments. Pastor Noble wasn't aware that this was going on in Phyllis' life so his words about not paying attention to the signs was very comforting and affirming to Phyllis. After Pastor Noble prayed, Phyllis recalls that she passed some urine and Carol Dudgeon believed Phyllis was being healed.

When Bruce came to pick up Phyllis, she could hardly contain her excitement. "God is healing me!" Bruce returned her to the Toronto Western Hospital and her next set of tests. Her signs were at the same levels. Disappointment settled in.

After a couple of weeks of no further changes Bruce said in his heart, "God, if you're not going to heal her don't wave the carrot in front of our noses."

Against despair, Phyllis continued to expect. She prayed, "God I believe you've done something special in my body but you are soon going to have to show the others."

Looking back, Phyllis felt like it was a cocky kind of prayer and she had overstepped her boundaries.

A few days later she received a phone call from her doctor. There was a donated kidney available for her.

She needed to get to the hospital right away.

CHAPTER 9
Transplant

The post-surgery fog began to lift and the first moments of clarity after surgery signaled the fact that something very good had happened - very, very good. She felt new life in her body. She could sense it immediately.

Phyllis remembered that Bruce had arrived on the ward just before she was taken in for surgery. His discovery of her hastily scribbled note on their kitchen table, "Gone to get a kidney. Love, Phyllis" had summoned Bruce to the hospital. She recalled seeing his face and knowing that they were about to begin a new life together. He had a slight smile, and the typical Bruce Fisher calmness. They squeezed hands. She can't remember if they kissed but just having him there gave her reassurance.

It's difficult to describe the exact feelings of going into a surgery that could begin - or end - your life. However she felt no fear and had a deep sense of peace and believed this was part of the effects of prayer.

Nurses told Bruce that there wasn't much more that he could do so he went home. A man from the church they attended came over to be with Bruce and they watched the Saturday night hockey game on CBC while Phyllis was going through surgery.

Phyllis' impression that something amazing happened was confirmed by the recovery room nurse who was standing at the foot of her bed. She was Jamaican and her beaming white smile said it all. Dr. Thompson, her surgeon, arrived on her ward and his first words were, "Oh Phyllis, it's a miracle! It's working like a racehorse."

How very comforting to Phyllis to wake up and to hear those words. She would be in isolation for the next ten days so her physician's comments gave her hope and sustained her until she could have contact with Bruce again.

Word of Phyllis' transplant generated widespread attention. It was quite remarkable. Doctors in residency who worked with kidney transplants, repeatedly poked their heads into Phyllis's room and enthused, "Hi, miracle girl!"

The hand of God was on her. Phyllis was humbly overjoyed with God's favor.

She never expected anything less.

One afternoon her nurse asked Phyllis if she would like some time to be alone. She swung her legs over the bed, relaxed for the first time and found her Bible. The first page she turned to was in the book of First Peter. The words she read became her life message.

They referred to the result of the testing of faith coming out like pure gold.

1 Peter 1:6-8 – "In all this you greatly rejoice, though now for a little while you may have had to suffer grief in all kinds of trials. These have come so that the proven genuineness of your faith—of greater worth than gold, which perishes even though refined by fire—may result in praise, glory and honor when Jesus Christ is revealed."

She had something better than gold.

She had a future.

Life as a transplant patient was truly uneventful. God blessed Phyllis with a normal life. She could do anything she wanted, and all she had to do was take 2 1/2 pills every day for thirty plus years.

Phyllis was sobered by the fact that someone else died in order for her to receive this kidney. In those days there was no sharing of donor information so Phyllis never knew who donated a kidney to her.

The transplanted kidney was a precious gift from God.

She determined to use the gift of life given to her for the glory of Jesus Christ.

CHAPTER 10
Pastoring – Part 1

No, she was not dreaming.

Pinching herself did not change the reality that she was now a pastor's wife. Bruce's first pastoral role as an assistant to Rev. George Ewald in Kingston, Ontario meant that she was a bona fide pastor's wife.

If anyone sincerely loved being the wife of a pastor it was Phyllis – and no one filled the role better.

Phyllis practiced attentiveness to others – not as a discipline but as an expression of her calling.

When Phyllis and Bruce were assisting in Kingston, she was in a Bible study and felt impressed that she would be used in the gifts of the Holy Spirit. That left her petrified because that function was such a high calling.

Phyllis began to use the gift of prophecy - speaking words of encouragement and admonition during church services as she was prompted by the Holy Spirit. To her, speaking a message in tongues and the necessity of having that interpreted meant there would have to be two gifts used. It just seemed easier to be used in one gift like giving a message of encouragement.

During times of singing and worship she would be prompted to give a word of encouragement. How could people hear her soft voice? For some reason things got quiet and her voice was the only one that was heard. That helped her feel that she was doing what God wanted her to do.

"The very fact that I didn't have a strong voice and yet I was heard, made the experiences feel favored by God. I didn't feel like I had to shout, just simply use the same type of voice you would if you were behind a pulpit."

It seemed that things got quiet when somebody audibly spoke in tongues. Automatically people got quiet waiting for the interpretation. When she gave a message she'd feel nervous and think, "I'm the only one speaking."

The Bible says that these gifts are not toys. They are gifts of love.

Phyllis describes being used by the Holy Spirit as feeling a prompting to go and say something to another person or engage them in conversation. In church. Or in the neighborhood.

A word from the Lord settled on her like an anointing. "The greatest thing you can give people is love. Ministry doesn't require a piano or a voice."

Congregants loved Phyllis because she was approachable, real and unconventional. She was as comfortable with sinners as with saints. She could easily relate to sinners. Her ministry was hallmarked by reaching beyond traditional barriers.

She inspired other young women to feel like they could succeed in ministry and life as well.

Rev. Hannah Price - one of Phyllis' role models – used to jokingly say about pastors' wives, "The men get paid; we do it for Jesus."

LYTTLETON – The Fishers' First Solo Pastorate
In 1971 the Pentecostal congregation in Lyttleton, New Brunswick invited Bruce to become their pastor. This was quite an honor as he was new to ministry and the congregation, though small in number, had a long track record of gifted pastors, as well as a highly regarded ministry. Phyllis was a newly married young wife of twenty-three. She felt humbled by the responsibility.

Lyttleton had one garage, a mom and pop store and a good-sized Baptist church just down the road from the Pentecostal one. For a rural town it was highly impacted by the Gospel. The Lyttleton congregation did their best to support the Fishers, however the monthly salary needed to be supplemented with eggs and produce from the congregation.

In many churches there is a real lack of male presence. Not Lyttleton. When you walked into that church you knew that it was a man's church. There were solid male role models for young men to look up to. Bruce became one of them.

Lyttleton ended up being not only a place of ministry, it also became a place of friendship. A few of the families in the congregation were the Fishers' age and just starting their families. Phyllis led a Bible study for the young moms. It wasn't long before each woman renewed her commitment to following Jesus. A good deal of time was spent praying for their mates – fine family men – but not devoted to God. Phyllis encouraged the women to expect God to do something special for their husbands. Their prayers in faith came to fruition in a way that changed the entire congregation.

It was in Lyttleton that Bruce and Phyllis experienced one of the most memorable moments in their ministry. Part way through a Sunday evening service, Bruce interrupted the flow of the service and told everyone, "I feel God wants anybody who will come forward for prayer to come to the Lord and get close to Him." The first one to respond was the husband of a woman who attended the Bible study. That husband was followed by many more of the men whose wives attended the Bible study. An unusual number of people responded to the call to renew their faith that night. It was a euphoric time.

Many people came to the Lord in the community during their time in Lyttleton. Some had heavy drinking problems. The congregation opened their church and their hearts to them in support.

SAINT JOHN – New Ministries
In 1974 the Fishers were invited to Saint John, New Brunswick and Bethany Church. Though Phyllis knew moving to Saint John was what God wanted for them, it was difficult for her. She was leaving friends and a church in Lyttleton that was

sincere in wanting God's Spirit to work in their lives.

Bethany was different. People seemed to feel, "If God was going to move he's not going to move in Saint John." The congregation in Bethany didn't see themselves as a place of outreach or a strong force in the community.

Phyllis had a new struggle to work through. She looked to the Lord for direction.

"Lord, what can I do to help this church?"

She heard the word, "Children."

The church hosted a program for elementary-aged boys and girls. Phyllis took charge of the girls group and loved them and the group grew. At the end of the semester a banquet was held for the parents and the children. Over one hundred parents and kids showed up and at least seventy-five percent of them were not church attenders.

In their second summer the Fishers started what they called "Drive In" services. They secured permission to use the parking lot of the local mall. A flatbed truck provided the platform for musicians to lead worship and Bruce to preach. The novelty of the plan attracted crowds. On a summer Sunday night you might see thirty people in church. Drive-in Church attracted over one hundred. People could participate in the service as they wished from the comfort of their car.
Good things were happening.

Phyllis remembers, "There were many wonderful young couples

that started working so very hard in that church to see it grow. I felt that if anybody learned how to change it was myself. You're not always going to find what you want or what you hope to see but I guess really stepping out in faith and in doing what you feel you can, will touch the community."

Some of the women started a bus ministry – providing transportation for community children to come to Sunday School. One of the buses was nicknamed *"Charlie Brown"* and the smaller bus was *"Peanuts".* Often they would literally run in to the homes on a Sunday morning and help the children get dressed so they could go to Sunday School. During the week women knitted mittens and other cozzy items so that the children would be warm for the winter.

A young woman by the name of Ann Harding and Phyllis would do follow up work. They would go out and visit the families of these children so that they would get to know what the church was about and people would get to know Ann and Phyllis as well.

There was a special communion service for the women in Bethany. One particular lady always spoke so highly of the previous pastor and his wife. Phyllis felt that lady implied that she was not as good or as loveable as the previous pastor's wife. So Phyllis chose the time as they were about to have communion to tell the lady how she felt. The other woman was shocked because she hadn't intended that meaning at all. In that moment all the hurt melted away. The woman, Judy Munn and her husband Ted would prove to be ever so kind to the Fishers for the remainder of their time at Bethany.

Volunteers in Bethany worked very hard. They were young couples with kids at home and they gave so much to the church to make it a success. The kind of dedication and potential that grew in Bethany was a pleasure and a lifetime memory for Phyllis to witness.

CHAPTER 11
Parenting

Adaptable was an apt descriptor of Phyllis.

Growing up she adapted to many homes and families. As a pastor's wife it didn't matter to Phyllis about the size of church or congregation or parsonage - she would adapt.

When she was told she couldn't have her own children - she adapted by adopting.

In Lyttleton their thoughts turned to having a family.

In 1972 Phyllis became mother to her son Shawn. Her gifts as a mom were evident immediately and she couldn't wait to receive her daughter, Robyn in 1975.

Phyllis took hold of her home and welded four unrelated-by-blood members into the loving family that she presided over to her death.

Phyllis was so proud of the people that Shawn and Robyn have become.

With equal enthusiasm, she embraced the arrival of grandsons Kaiden and Ryland, then later, granddaughters Hailey and Hannah.

Who could have ever imagined that this family would come into being and be glued together by the love and encouragement of this extraordinary lady besought by illness most of her life.

Phyllis had extra motivation to create a home where unconditional love was the norm. Not that there weren't clearly defined and enforced behavioural rules. But she wanted her children to know that they would always be loved because of who they were and that Bruce and Phyllis would always be there together for them. She knew full well that children from a broken home face the monsters of abandonment and rejection.

For decades she filtered everything in her life through the effects of abandonment from her own childhood.

"Words take on different meanings for people who have been abandoned as a child. Even the simple fact that someone may not say 'hello' or may even say it but in a tone that may sound dismissive can be so hurtful to an unwanted child."

Phyllis appreciated the courage it takes for a woman to allow their child to be adopted - to place their child in another's hands.

Shawn was a young adult when his birth mother called to wish him a happy birthday. She asked if they could get together.

Phyllis readily agreed though she had to fight through her feelings of abandonment. Not that his birth mother was a threat but the thought entered her mind, "What if he picked her over me?"

Both Shawn and Robyn only had eyes for Phyllis.

CHAPTER 12
Pastoring – Part 2

MONCTON – Mrs. Bailey's Prayers
In 1978 the Fishers accepted the call to pastor a church in Moncton, New Brunswick.

During their time there, David Mainse's national Christian TV program, *100 Huntley Street*, needed local volunteers to follow up those that had come to a place of faith or were interested in wanting to learn more. They needed people to go visit particularly what was called "along the shore" - the French communities like Shediac - along the coast of New Brunswick.

Phyllis volunteered, even though she knew no French. Fortunately for her there was a wonderful lady – Mrs. Bailey, who was in her 60's - with a French background and who spoke French. They went into homes together.

The first time they drove away from the Bible study Mrs. Bailey turned to Phyllis with tears streaming down her face and said, "Mrs. Fisher I have prayed for 30 years for this incredible move of the Holy Spirit."

People invited their relatives to come to the studies. Attendance flourished.

For a long time the women attending the Bible study didn't know Phyllis was a pastor's wife. She was there to represent 100 Huntley Street, a daily Christian television program, not to represent her church. Then one day she hosted a luncheon in their parsonage and one of the ladies said, "Your husband is a pastor!" The secret was out and they began to laugh so hard.

Without any pressure from Phyllis, twenty to twenty-five people from the study started to attend their church on Sunday nights. Phyllis continued with her ministry in that area. Eventually two churches additional were planted in the same area. Phyllis was invited to the opening of one of the churches - a very special honor for her.

Phyllis never took any credit for the results because in her words, "it had nothing to do with who I was. It was all them. When we would leave they would literally say please come back and tell us more. Nobody could create that situation. It wasn't myself - it was God."

MONTREAL – Multi-cultural Heaven
In January 1983 they were invited to lead Evangel Church, in downtown Montreal.

Phyllis and Bruce carried a passion for ministry around the world through their entire ministry. In moving to Montreal the world came to them. They were now living and worshiping with people of all cultures and backgrounds. The church was blessed with many people from the Philippines, Poland, Russia, the Middle East and particularly the Caribbean Islands as well as other nations.

All of their daughter Robyn's friends were either from Africa or the West Indies. Phyllis was teaching Robyn's Sunday School class. Then she found out there were young men ages 15 to 18 needing a Sunday School teacher so she volunteered. Shawn and a French boy were the only two white boys in the class. Phyllis recalls how on one Sunday one of them left the class to go get a drink of water and one of the other young men jokingly said, "One down, one to go." There was a healthy camaraderie between the different cultures.

One of their most memorable experiences in Montreal was after a Sunday service, when a woman, who worked as a chambermaid in a hotel, put her arms around Phyllis and told her she was so glad that Bruce and Phyllis were in Evangel because people could feel Bruce and Phyllis' love for them.

EDMONTON – Righting A Sinking Ship

In 1990 they accepted the call to Central Tabernacle. Central had a reputation as a flagship of the Pentecostal Assemblies of Canada – one of Canada's largest church facilities and congregations. Four General Superintendents came out of Central. Well known pastors with last names like McAlister, Buntain, Johnstone, Taitinger, MacKnight, Johnson and Upton preceded the Fishers.

Two years previous to their arrival the church had experienced a traumatic split that eviscerated the congregation. The bleeding still hadn't stopped after twenty-four months.

Bruce accepted the call that other leaders had turned down. The church was in a tough situation. Phyllis remembers praying with people around the altar on Sunday nights. The people were so broken because of the split.

Bruce poured his heart and soul into bringing healing to the congregation. A chorus that was sung on many Sundays contained the lyrics, "Pour your healing oil through me, like a river of love, pour your healing from above."

Before long, Bruce would be in need of his own healing.

Being in ministry came with its rewards and challenges, some self-inflicted.

Phyllis recalls with deep sadness, hearing the sound of Shawn's footpads on the kitchen floor as he said to his dad, "Do you have to go again, daddy?"

"I believed great pastors and their wives are always on the go - always away from home all the time."

Phyllis felt that if Bruce's car was in the driveway more than one night a week that was too much.

Somewhere around mid-1992 Bruce was not feeling well. Thinking that the symptoms must have something to do with recovering from heart surgery, he went to his physician. The doctor said the source wasn't physical and sent him to a psychologist. The psychologist then sent him to a psychiatrist.

The psychiatrist told him that he had never seen anyone so deep in a burnout as Bruce was.

Bruce was surprised. He didn't feel like he was burned out. He felt tired.

He continued to feel "fuzzy in his thinking." He began to have a difficult time crafting messages, and being focused. There was no ability any longer to do what he had done for decades.

He still loved ministry - he just couldn't do it anymore.

It was an anxious time for both of them. If Bruce could no longer be a pastor what would Phyllis do? A pastor's wife belonged to a church family only as long as their spouse was the pastor. So many of Phyllis' social connections in Edmonton were at Central Tabernacle. What would she do?

CHAPTER 13
Chaplaincy

Four years prior, in September 1990, Phyllis had taken the first step in the direction of her dream. Phyllis had long envisioned herself serving as a chaplain.

She started a two-year chaplaincy program. The basic levels were completed at the Misericordia Hospital, the Royal Alexandra Hospital, and the University of Alberta in Edmonton. She worked for a whole year at the University of Alberta Hospital as an intern/resident. A strong emphasis on pastoral care was woven through the curriculum. Phyllis received her bachelors and later her Masters in theological studies at St. Stephen's College - a faculty of the U of A.

When Phyllis was in residency at the University of Alberta they were writing up reports on transplant patients. The media seemed more interested in current transplant patients than they were in patients who had long-term transplants. She always felt that a donor would probably be interested in knowing the longevity of the success of transplants, like Phyllis' experience.

Phyllis connected with people who were ill, and waiting for a donor. They were genuinely excited when they learned about the longevity of her and other patients' transplant experiences.

Upon graduation Phyllis volunteered for six months at the provincial prison in Fort Saskatchewan. With opportunity came challenges. Learning to trust herself in new situations was a difficult challenge. Once again her child experience of abandonment threatened to sabotage her career before it even started. The phrase "what if" came very easily to her mind and nothing good ever followed that thought.

Phyllis didn't want to miss out on life because she was fixated on the theme of rejection or abandonment. She coached herself intentionally to not be deterred from engaging with other people in a group because she may misunderstand what is being said or even if she was actually welcomed by the group. She pushed through those fears and made herself a valuable contributor.

After some well-earned initial success, Phyllis decided to upgrade her skills by taking a course on prison ministry in Spring Hill, Nova Scotia.

There, many of her professors had backgrounds in the United Church, the Reformed church, Baptist churches and Catholic churches. The organizers of the course expressed initial concerns that Phyllis, being Pentecostal, might find the leanings of the professors "different" than what she would expect. But Phyllis' broad religious background made the environment that she was learning in very comfortable and familiar.

Phyllis became a certified chaplain in 1994.

It was a bittersweet time because her certification coincided with Bruce's resignation as the lead pastor of Central Tabernacle.

Bruce had just gone on long-term disability. This was an extremely difficult period for both of them. His beloved career was ending just as Phyllis' chaplaincy career was beginning.

The timing was providential for Phyllis because without the chaplaincy ministry she's not sure what they would've done for sufficient income and significance.

While it was a time of grieving over Bruce's health and the loss of his career, they found solace in the way God had initially led them to Alberta.

When Bruce had his triple bypass in December 1989, chaplains visited him in the Montreal General Hospital. Phyllis was there and their conversation turned to Alberta. The told her Alberta was the hotbed for Chaplaincy And Pastoral Education (CAPE) training. Both Edmonton and Calgary offered CAPE training to a higher degree than any other province in Canada. Phyllis had always wanted to be a chaplain. She tucked this vital piece of information in the top drawer of the back of her mind.

The Board of Central Tabernacle had invited Bruce and Phyllis to come as their pastors in the fall of 1989 and they declined that invitation.

When Central offered them a second invitation in May 1990 they felt it was God's will for them and they accepted.

Little did they know that moving to Edmonton to become

pastors at Central would also provide the possibility of training for Phyllis and then an opportunity to serve as a chaplain.

The winter of 1994, Bruce and Phyllis built a cottage/home at Sunnyside Camp on Sylvan Lake, Alberta and moved there in September 1995. Bruce fixed watches and grandfather clocks. Phyllis applied for a job in Ponoka at the Alberta Psychiatric Brain Injury Hospital.

Going for a job interview was so intense for her.

She felt weak in interviews. The interviewer had all the control. She had lost the job in her mind before she even showed up for the interview. Phyllis appeared confident - and she was - but if she was challenged she was easily crushed.

An over sensitivity to rejection was woven through her life – in some ways it was the theme of her life.

But she got the job in Ponoka.

And she loved it.

Phyllis taught every other week in the substance-abuse group. She ministered to people with brain injuries, substance abuse, or mental illness.

Her previous volunteer work in the provincial prison had showed Phyllis that many of the inmates had some form of mental illness. Those interactions helped prepare her for a fulfilling thirteen-year career in Ponoka.

Typical of her interactions with patients was a man whose mother had recently died. Phyllis enquired if he wanted to talk. "Yes." They picked up coffee at Tim Horton's and went to a park. Phyllis remembers him turning to her and asking, "Phyllis, do you think that my mother even knew I existed?"

Phyllis answered by referring to Bible verses about how God likens Himself to a mother. Mothers cannot forget their children. Even Jesus talked about that in the New Testament. And she assured him that even though his mother may not have been able to visit him, just because he was her child he would be so stamped in her heart that it would be impossible for her to forget him. His whole countenance brightened from her reassuring words.

As a chaplain Phyllis was able to encourage and empathize with patients who were facing their own organ transplants. She spoke with patients who were afraid to have a transplant and when she explained how long she'd had her transplant they happily responded, "You have been how long?"

Phyllis' desire was that people would know that transplants work.

On the 30th anniversary of her transplant, Phyllis sent her picture to the Toronto Western Hospital – where her surgery happened. She was acknowledged and celebrated for getting to thirty years as a transplant patient. The honor and celebration were for her about encouraging other people, not about her. A letter of congratulations from Jocelyn meant the world to her.

One of her sweetest, and sacred occasions was when she shared communion with patients at the hospital. She had the patients come to the front and form a semi-circle. They served communion to one another. She wanted to emphasize that the cross makes us all equal. She told the patients, "We're here ministering to one another."

Phyllis explained the group that if Jesus could pick one place to come and serve communion he would pick their place. The look on their faces was indicative of how special they felt and holding the service with their help made them feel special in the eyes of God. Serving one another and everyone feeling equal was the strength that Phyllis to that moment.

Chaplaincy was everything to her but in 1995 Phyllis' poison counts started creeping higher.

Five years later her doctor advised her that she might have two more years left with the transplanted kidney. From 1969 on she'd had clear sailing so the prognosis was unexpected and disappointing.

She felt so angry.

Here she was, holding down a job as a chaplain, and working on her Masters. "I was a mother and a grandmother and I thought when I looked out at other people who looked so much sicker than me, I felt like, 'I'll show you.'

"Sometimes anger is good because it makes you fight."

In 2002 she was forced back onto dialysis.
Between 2002 and 2006 it was difficult for Phyllis to look at the

clock and know that she had to leave the work she loved to go on the dialysis machine. Her treatments began in Red Deer and then she was sent to Wetaskiwin.

She was on dialysis three days a week - Monday, Wednesday and Friday. On Thursday she didn't work so that gave her a bit of a breather between dialysis treatments. On Tuesdays she was able to put in a full day of work.

Colleagues would joke with her saying, "Who looks forward to working a whole day?"

And Phyllis would say, "If you're on dialysis you do."

CHAPTER 14
A Second Kidney Donor

Karen McLeod was employed as a social worker at Alberta Hospital in Ponoka where Phyllis was a chaplain. She didn't know Phyllis but they shared a mutual friend in Caroline Taylor.

When the subject of Phyllis needing a kidney came up, Karen couldn't shake the conversation from her mind. On her hour long drive home from work she mulled over how she could do something to help.

"My blood type is 'O positive.' I imagine anybody could use my kidney."

She bounced the idea off Caroline at work the next day. "You know I'm thinking about donating my kidney to Phyllis. What do you think? Do you think that Phyllis would be OK with that? I know she knows lots of people. Do you think that she'd want a kidney from me?"

Caroline rolled her eyes, "Oh, come on. Of course she would

take your kidney. I mean hello, you know that they're not dropping off the ceiling."

Karen was sincerely worried that Phyllis wouldn't want her kidney because they weren't related and she didn't know anything about Karen. So she asked Caroline if she would share the idea with Phyllis. She didn't want to be present. "You let me know what she says."

Caroline reported back that it was more than fine with Phyllis.

"OK, let's do it!"

Protocol was for donors and recipients to be kept separate through the process. The transplant physician met with Phyllis and Karen together. Doctors don't usually connect with the donors and recipients together.

There was blood work and in Karen's words "a bazillion tests" to do. Surgeons advised Karen on the risks and the pain she would face. Pain? "I thought to myself as long as it's not any more painful than getting a gallbladder out the old way because that was not much fun for six weeks. I thought OK, if it's like that I can do it."

Once the match was confirmed and they got through all the testing, the specialists wanted assurance that Karen wasn't feeling pressured to be a donor because she and Phyllis worked together.

Karen wrote a letter to the surgeon, Dr. Gary Schenkel, informing him that her kidney belonged to Phyllis. No pressure at all. Just pleasure at being able to do something good.

She felt like a surrogate mother. "In a way I was carrying a baby for somebody else. That's where it didn't matter to me if the transplant was good for two weeks or two months or two decades. The kidney was hers and I was prepared to go forward."

"I sent the letter in and I guess that must've done the trick because once they know that the donor's OK and they know you're willing to give the kidney no matter what, then they're prepared to go forward."

Then they had to patiently wait an entire year for the surgery.

During the waiting period Karen was driving on the highway, back-and-forth to Ponoka every day. Worried that she might be involved in a car accident, she posted little notes in her car.

"THIS KIDNEY BELONGS TO PHYLLIS FISHER."

There was a phone number attached for the benefit of police or ambulance workers. Friends would get in her car and they'd quizzically enquire what the notes were all about.

"I don't have my own children and I have never cared for a child but it felt like I was giving somebody else life. It was just so important to protect that kidney for me. It was precious cargo."

Reflecting on her choice to be an organ donor, Karen says, "That was the best thing I ever did in my life."

CHAPTER 15
Caroline, Karen & Phyllis

Caroline Taylor, Karen McLeod, Phyllis and two other women – Lynn and Lorna, colleagues in Ponoka - were known as the "Sunshine Ladies." I spent an afternoon listening in on Phyllis, Caroline and Karen's conversation over tea in Phyllis' living room. March 23, 2017 was a cold day outside but things warmed up quickly inside. The three friends hadn't seen each other in months and their giggles, laughter, squeals, hugs and tears communicated as much as their words.

CAROLINE: I started at Alberta Hospital in Ponoka - now called Centennial Centre - in 1999. The brain injury unit was where I met Phyllis.

I was asked to be a patient advocate on the unit. I wasn't certain how I would ever do that role because I didn't know the layout of the area. The unit was new and I was feeling very lost. So I thought, "Chaplains are helpful. That's what they do. I'll go to the chaplain's office." So I stopped in. Phyllis was in a long flowing skirt and she was so gracious and had so much flare.

Of course it was easy to talk with Phyllis and get to know who she was and she said she knew who my dad was because he came to the Centre and played music sometimes. She was so consoling. And we had the bond of a shared faith in Jesus. That was the beginning and after that we started to get to know each other more and more.

PHYLLIS: In 2002 I had to go back on dialysis. I would drive for treatments from Ponoka to Wetaskiwin. Caroline would meet me in Wetaskiwin and we'd get a Tim's together.

Four years later my transplanted kidney was crashing. Its harrowing looking back and observing yourself going through a serious illness in your twenty's and then once again going through renal failure, this time in your fifty's.

CAROLINE: When I realized that Phyllis' kidney was crashing and she needed help I said to her very bluntly "Phyllis you're dying" and she said, "Yes, I am."

I said "We've got to get you a kidney" and Phyllis said, "Well at my age I'm not on anybody's list and I'm an only child. I have adopted children and nobody is a match."

I said, "If I was a match I would give you a kidney today. I mean, I would be so happy to do that. We've got to find you one. And we will!"

Phyllis said, "Well I just can't go up to somebody and say, 'Oh, what's your blood type. I need a kidney'."

I told Phyllis, "You can't do that but I can and I will start talking to anybody I want."

And I did I start talking to everybody and anybody. I knew people that I thought might have an inclination toward that kind of charity. I just kept talking it up and then all of a sudden there was Karen McLeod. I told her about Phyllis.

KAREN: So the next day I came in to work and I said to Caroline, "You know I've had a long chat with myself and I thought about it this morning and I think I'll go ahead and see if I'm a match for Phyllis. So do you think it'll be OK?

And Caroline gave me this look like, "You numbskull" but she didn't actually say that. She just said, "Of course Phyllis is gonna be OK with it."

So I said to Caroline, "Why don't you go talk to Phyllis first and then you come back and tell me what she says. Then I'll go in because I want to make sure that its OK with her."

CAROLINE: I was amazed at the quickness of Karen's decision. I know that people think about this kind of decision for months sometimes. But there was an emergency here. We both saw Phyllis changing and just getting so tired. We both knew Phyllis couldn't carry this on much longer. And to have Karen's decision immediately was just phenomenal.

The three of us had to do a few trips to Edmonton for interviews and tests. They were frustrating times. I was thinking, "Why are they being so silly waiting and waiting? Can't we just get on with it." I was on cloud nine and overwhelmed and it didn't matter how tired I got driving. I didn't even mind because this was so exciting and it was so worthwhile and I just felt like this was God's hand.

My husband Ken was so supportive. It didn't matter how many days or how many hours or what time or anything. If it was about Phyllis it was a green light from him for me to go do it.

KAREN: Caroline was the glue that kept us together. No one knows the amount of time Caroline put in to take care of Phyllis.

I am so grateful to Phyllis because I felt like she made me a better person.

There was the time Phyllis convinced me to talk to my mother. I hadn't talked to her in nearly thirty years.

I was visiting in Monterreo and decided to go to a monastery. Prayer candles could be purchased so I selected two - one candle for my brother-in-law and one candle for my mother. They were going through hard times. However, I couldn't get the candles to stand up. One of the attendants told me that I was standing the candles in the wrong place – it was in the place for those who were dead.

When I arrived back home I felt I should contact my mom while she was still alive. So, I went to visit her in Cape Breton. We reconciled our differences. I owe that to Phyllis.

CAROLINE: The dialysis treatments were such a God thing. I hated blood or vomit or even touching someone else's skin. But I was able to help Phyllis with no issues.

PHYLLIS: Caroline would rub my toes as the treatments were done.

CAROLINE: There are not many people who have the will and drive to carry on like Phyllis. She would get painful needles with composure. I can't help but talk about the tenacity that Phyllis had to carry on with some of the surgeries. They would do two or three a day sometimes.

Dr. Sapijaszko (who was treating Phyllis for skin cancer) said, "I don't know how much longer her life can go on." He would be amazed to know that Phyllis still living. His forecast wasn't that promising and we were frustrated by him sometimes.

PHYLLIS: We proved him wrong.

KAREN: Yes, we did!

CAROLINE: Through those years Phyllis was still forging ahead. She was studying and she finished her Masters degree. When she graduated, Bruce put on this adorable formal dinner. The programs that he had printed, everything was just exquisite and he said, "She's worth it, she's worked hard."

We all knew Phyllis had worked hard but even then she was in distress. But she rose above it.

KAREN: Caroline, bless her heart, she did it all. She took both of us to all the appointments and I was such a wreck because I never drove in downtown Edmonton.

The day before the surgery, Caroline was driving me again. And

I said to her, "You know, I'm just thinking that something bad might happen. I might die during surgery."

If I don't live let Phyllis and Bruce know this, especially Bruce because I know he's going to feel guilty. Tell him, "You didn't get me roped into this. It's something that I choose to do and as long as Phyllis gets the kidney, that's all that counts. So don't feel bad about it."

When it was time to get prepped for the surgery you're all by yourself and you're waiting to get those horrible stockings on and all the other stuff. I remember Caroline came to see me. I would expect her to come and give me some wishes but I heard this voice and I thought, "Holy moly, there's somebody else here that I know."

Bruce came to see ME.

PHYLLIS: I teased a friend of Robyn's about Karen's colorful vocabulary and how I would inherit that propensity with her kidney.

KAREN: In the beginning when we were signing up for the rooms I was able to get a private room because I had a good medical coverage. The lady said, "Well you know we often save all the private rooms for people who are palliative so you know you'll probably get a double room."

So when I came out of recovery and they were wheeled me down, I'm coming into a room with nobody in it and I'm like, "Oh my gosh the surgery didn't go as well as I thought. I'm really dying."

I get in there and I was so worried. I thought "Oh my gosh, my worst fears." Then Caroline came in and I said that to her and she's like rolling her eyes and saying, "This is your room."

I said, 'No, it can't be my room. Look," I said, "there's already flowers here. There's red roses and these can't be for me. These flowers belong to someone else. Nobody would get me roses."

And Caroline said, "No, there's a card on them. They're from Bruce."

KAREN: Phyllis and I were in recovery for about five days and of course in different rooms. And Bruce would come to visit me. And he shared with me emails that he had gotten from friends. They said they're hoping Phyllis was doing well and they mentioned me as well. It was so encouraging to hear that. I got copies of the emails from him and I put them in a book. Their sentiment really helped me.

They were praying that we would both recover and do well.

It was just so nice to be a part of helping Phyllis live. She made me so happy because she was able to live see the births of two more grandchildren.

PHYLLIS: My grandson Ryland thanked Karen for helping his gramma.

We all thanked Karen and Caroline for helping Phyllis.

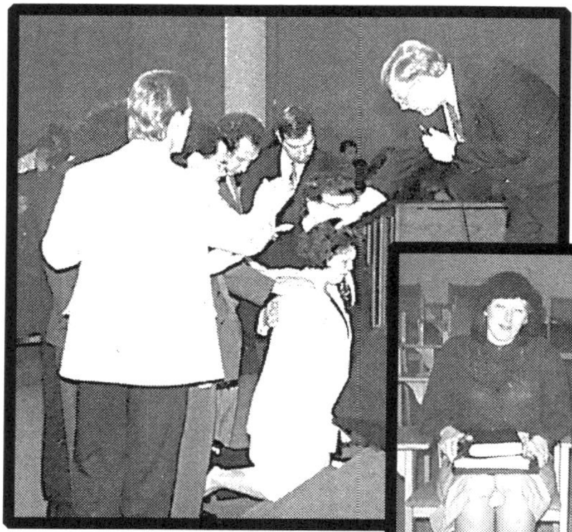
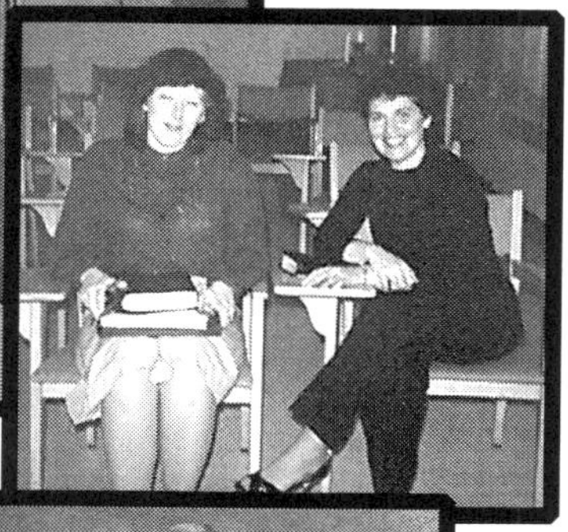
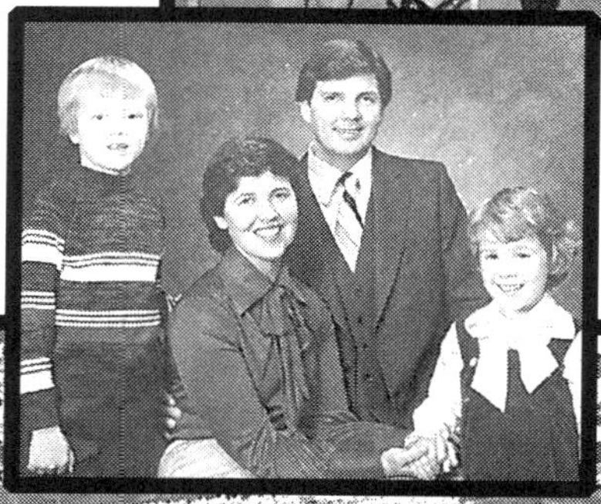
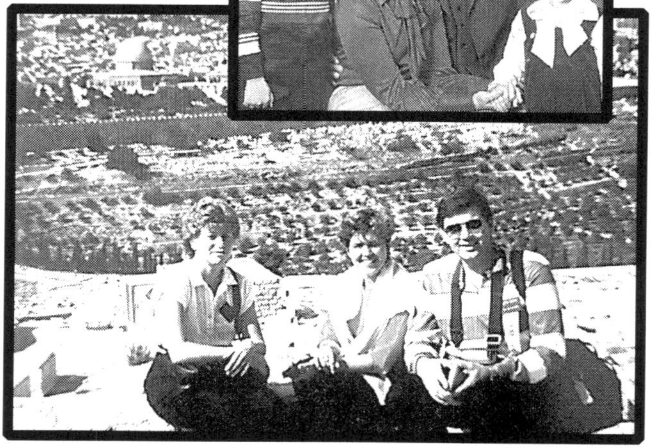

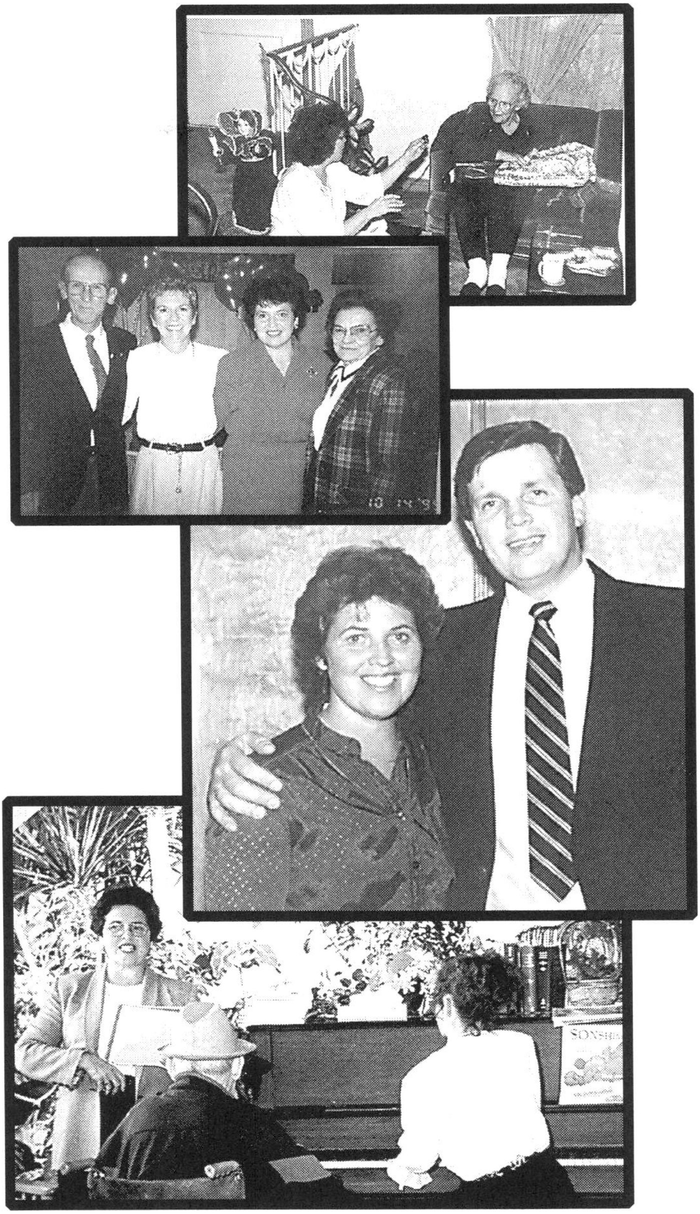

CHAPTER 16
The Big Talk

When the skin grafts would not take that her doctor said to her it's time now for "the big talk."

Dr. Olson met with Bruce and Phyllis in his office at the U of A hospital.

Surgery was no longer an option.

And if she got an infection it would result in amputation.

The wound care was not improving the situation.

"Gradually we will run out of options," he told them. "We both know this is coming and there's only so much that surgery could do."

They began to talk about the inevitability of death.

The emotional shock surprised her.

She knew going in to the consult the subject would be about death and she felt prepared for that because she had thought through it a lot. When she actually heard the words they had a deeper effect on her than she imagined they would.

The reality of death impacted her deeply.

Hearing her impending death articulated by someone other than herself was quite unsettling.

Phyllis' initial reaction was deep sadness. Her body, that God had blessed so many times, had betrayed her - let her down.

Her doctor told her, "You'd be surprised how many people have said that."

It seemed that she had conquered so much since 1969. The feeling that with God's help she could beat anything that her body faced was part of her thinking.

She didn't feel that God had betrayed her at this moment. She just felt disappointed that the recovery she had in the past wasn't going to be available in the future.

Phyllis reflected on the fact that because she'd been involved in ministry and helped other people who were facing death she was surprised at her own reaction. She felt her experience would temper the emotion. Not so.

The idea of her facing death - her own death - made her realize how attached we are to life on earth and how faith is so vital in facing the stark realities of life and death.

People facing a similar prognosis don't need to feel apologetic for those kind of feelings because God has put within us a remarkable desire to live.

That winter she wasn't feeling good and she asked her doctor if she should go out to BC for Christmas to be with Shawn and Kristin. He said to her, "If you were my mother I would want you there for Christmas." So off to BC went Bruce and Phyllis for one more Christmas with the kids.

When they returned in January she had a PET (Positron-emission tomography) and a CAT scan.

After the scans, her doctor came in and explained to her the prognosis of how long she had. This was the end of February. He told her that she had about six months to live. At most.

It was very quiet moment in the consultation room.

Bruce told Phyllis later that he couldn't believe how stoic she was when she heard the news.

In her heart was the thought - "the time has come."

On the drive home the conversation turned to death. They both knew this day was coming. Bruce said that even though they knew the time was coming it was still like a knife through his heart when he heard the doctor's words.

In the days following, Phyllis would have moments of quiet tears.

There was a time when Phyllis heard Robyn talking about an event that she and her friends would be going to some months in the future. It would be on Robyn's birthday. And it struck Phyllis that that date would be beyond the six-month timeframe. And she thought, "I won't be here."

She felt like she couldn't breathe let alone talk.

As were talking about that memory Phyllis chuckled at the fact that all her stoicism went right out the window. "In that moment, you're sitting there with your child and the deep sense of not wanting to let go. Of wanting to live. Of wanting to be there. But she also felt the pull of faith and the words of the hymn, "O the love that will not let me go."

The hymn is about the magnificent love of Jesus that pulls you to where you belong. Pulls you to Him, pulls you to turn your heart and mind to eternity and heaven.

Everything within us fights for life.

Faith tells us that death is like a baby going down the birth canal and what feels like death is actually a journey towards life. Feelings tell us death may not come that easy.

When given her prognosis, Phyllis didn't lay down and give up on her future. She didn't quit on life but she did recognize the reality of her impending passing.

In that moment, as a person of faith who believes in the resurrection and divine hope, that's when faith became all the more real. Phyllis said, "You grab hold of the situation and live in the now."

Within herself Phyllis prayed, "Oh God, walk with me."

She felt a peace within, an acquired peace - no lights or flashes, nothing stupendous - just a calm assurance.

Phyllis posted to her Facebook group that night - "I am not sure if the group receives this or not, just in case I will include Carol Dudgeon. I am so encouraged by all your notes, prayers, and songs. I had my Pastor's wife and a friend in to visit. Jocelyn Jones was our youth leader in Saint John, NB. So proud of her. Family tomorrow, and some friends. Bruce, is taking time off work, so he will be here with me. You know how he is, quiet, thinking and then surprises you. He told me tonight."

"Our family Dr. thinks I have three months. We will see my other surgeon Monday. Me, I feel like it will be longer. My oldest Grandson phoned and is going to try and come out and he said, "but Grandma has always beat it!" A nice gift of encouragement to receive from him. You folks are the best. I even heard from old high school buddy today from near Coby. It has been over forty years since we last saw one another. He always teased me about my faith, but not in a cruel way."

Phyllis went on - "I am so grateful for EPBC where we met and the wonderful influences we had on our lives. One night Brother Atter was in our home in Lyttleton, NB speaking at our Prayer Conference. I woke up in middle of the night and in his sleep he was talking in tongues. What an impact on a young pastor's wife! I. D. Raymer slept in our room while Bruce and I slept in our son's nursery in a 3/4 bed. A little cramped for

Bruce."

"I smile now as I picture it. Our home was blessed. Good night, and may the new day bless you and fill your hearts with new memories and learning to encourage you in the days to come." Love, Phyl.

Everybody must face the issue of death ultimately. However there's no pattern or expected or common way of facing death.

Phyllis was not afraid to die - it was the process of dying that troubled her. "I have had a lot of pain but no different than other people experienced.

She confided about her fear of pain. Her fear had nothing to do with a lack of faith, just the frailty of our human bodies and knowing what pain can feel like.

The doctors assured her that they would not allow her to suffer.

CHAPTER 16
When You Can't Come Back

Those who knew Phyllis best, esteemed her the most.

Family and friends clearly saw that she was tenacious, if not invincible. She overcame so much in her seven decades of life. Time after time the setbacks she faced were met with a matter-of-fact resolve to find a way forward, by taking one grace-filled step after another. She quarterbacked a lot of comebacks.

Years after her second transplant she was diagnosed with cancer. What does the Bible say about God not letting us be tempted beyond what we can bear? God must have believed Phyllis had Herculean shoulders to bear so much sorrow.

She was forced to have her parotid gland removed - a six-hour surgery. When the gland was removed it meant a large portion of the right side of her face was affected and she lost her muscle tone. The intensive surgery on her neck eventually caused full paralysis to the right side of her face. After the surgery Phyllis was able to see in a mirror a change in her appearance - the drooping of her eye, the drooping of her mouth - and eventually, the entire right side of her face.

Later, because of internal pressure, she lost the hearing in her right ear.

As a woman it's a natural thing to be conscious of your appearance. As a child, Phyllis was self-conscious about the size of her mouth. All through her life people would comment that they would know her smile anywhere. Phyllis felt in some way a little embarrassed by how large her smile was.

And now she would give anything to have that smile back.

Not to be deterred by being self-conscious she always found a way to be included discreetly in family photos.

Phyllis had subsequent surgery on both of her legs, which required numerous skin grafts. In between treatments she travelled to Ontario in 2015 to visit Coby and see her extended family and friends.

One more big surgery came in March 2016 and then surgery on her legs in June 2016. In between the surgeries was the radiation for her head and neck area.

In total, Phyllis had over one hundred and fifty-five radiation treatments. Because of the related damage her skin graphs were not taking.

Since the latest skin grafts did not take she was now down to bone in her legs. There was no skin to do any grafting on.

Doctors were also concerned that underneath the bone was more cancer that they could not get at. (Strangely enough there was skin on those places in the last month of Phyllis' life.)

It was at this time that Phyllis was growing weaker and beginning to think about death. She asked her lifelong friends since Bible College - a whole group of faithful people in her life - to pray for her. She rounded them up on Facebook. She so appreciated all of their prayers.

CHAPTER 18
An Appointment With God

"What if I am a disappointment to God?"

Her question came out of left field. In our last conversation Phyllis raised a question that was on her mind, "What if I'm a disappointment to God? What if I haven't lived a life worthy of him?"
Phyllis knew her time was coming quickly. She asked the questions not out of regret but out of a reverential awareness that she would soon be in God's presence and there's not a lot of time left to make up for what might have not been done in the past.

"Thinking about God and standing in His presence, you recognize that aside from the righteousness of Christ, I have nothing to offer God."

True humility is not thinking less about yourself but thinking about yourself less. Phyllis was a humble woman. Her entire life had been focused on others. It was ironic that she felt other famous Christians had so many more profound accomplishments than her. Her feelings of deficiency reflected humility more than reality.

Phyllis was amazed at how often people talk about heaven when they're dying. She reflected on a conversation she had with her friend Ruth Johnstone, whose husband Steve had passed away recently. Ruth told her that "when I get to heaven I can only imagine falling on my face and weeping."

Memories flooded in to Phyllis' mind about when she became a Christian and how it affected her as a child. She felt very aware of the love, and majesty, and holiness of God. It felt like it was too much for her to contain. She was awed by the holiness of God. Now she felt those same feelings of being unworthy of God loving her and Jesus dying for her.

When her father was dying many years earlier she had flown to Vancouver to visit him in hospital. She had not met her dad until that day.

"Mr. Ryan your daughter is here."

He said Phyllis's name and she remembers the feeling of hearing her father say her name for the first time.

It was like being called by someone special. The sound filled her with so much love and acceptance.

Jesus appeared to Mary Magdalene just after his resurrection. She thought he was the gardener. Everything changed when He called her name. Did Mary Magdalene recognize Jesus because of what she saw or because of what she heard?

Phyllis was settled by faith that she would hear Jesus call her name. Soon.

CHAPTER 19
Slipping The Bonds Of Earth

Over the last days of her life, Phyllis was in the care of physicians at the Grey Nuns Hospital in Edmonton. My wife Jocelyn and I had showed up to visit and pray with her. Moments later Bruce arrived. The nurse was settling Phyllis into a chair. Bruce called her, "Babe," excused himself in front us, leaned in and kissed Phyllis "hello."

Tender affection still alive after forty-nine years of marriage.

Phyllis was admitted into "tertiary" care at the Grey Nuns hospital on May 4th. Doctors did their best to keep her pain under control. Bruce visited her every day to enjoy their last moments together.

Shawn and Kristen and their boys, Robyn and her girls and Bruce and Phyllis spent a wonderful Mother's Day together. A fine meal, family photos and lots of laughter. They had already said their goodbyes on Easter weekend. That weekend Phyllis told each of the most precious people in her life - "Honor God with your life."

On Wednesday May 10th Jocelyn and I were in attendance at the evening service of the ABNWT District Conference. The worship team was singing the lyric, "You are good, you are good and your love endures." Bruce texted us that Phyllis was holding on and still conscious. The next day we visited Bruce and his "Babe."

On May 19Th we went to see Phyllis again at the Grey Nuns. Thirty-eight years previous, to the day, Pastor Bruce had officiated our wedding ceremony. The significance of the timing was not lost on us. God's providential care is often illustrated in seemingly co-incidental dates.

Bruce, Kristen, Shawn, Robyn and Robyn's daughters were there. Each of her granddaughters gave Phyllis a tender hug. We prayed together as a family.

On May 21st Bruce, Kristen, Shawn, Robyn met with me at the Grey Nuns. Phyllis had been sedated. There would be no more conversations with her – on earth.

I heard Bruce tell his children that their mom had faced every prognosis with resolve. "This is just the next thing to face."

Phyllis Ryan Fisher slipped the bounds of earth in the early hours of May 23, 2017.

She breathed heavenly air for the first time.

It would be no surprise at all if heaven's air had the familiar scent of her beloved Kawartha Lakes and the town of Coboconk – "Coby" to Phyl.

God has a way of making heaven feel like home, just like Phyllis made her home feel like heaven.

CHAPTER 20
See You In The Morning

What soap is for the body, tears are for the soul.

I have learned that if you follow your tears you will find your heart.

If you find your heart you'll see what's important to God.

If you see what's important to God you find the path forward in your life.

Death for a believer in Jesus is not a period at the end of life's sentence, it's a comma that punctuates life to a higher level.

Jesus said, "I am the resurrection and the life. The one who believes in me will live even though they die." John 11:26 (NIV)

Death is not "goodbye" – it's "goodnight, see you in the morning."

Bruce and I met and talked for 2 1/2 hours on June 19th. If you know Bruce and I, you know how profound that was. Our conversation focused on the feelings he was experiencing after Phyllis passed away.

"I know that her physical body is gone but it's the spiritual connection that is so hard to let go. As she was dying her spirit was just as vibrant as it always has been but her body wouldn't allow her to express that vibrancy. Her body was dying and she no longer could express herself as the Phyllis that everyone knew. But she was still the same Phyllis."

One night I was lying on the couch, I was sure I saw Phyllis out of the corner of my eye. I thought, 'Oh, she's coming out of the bedroom.' Of course she wasn't but the experience felt so real."

Brice shared, "As a pastor I've officiated at many funerals but I never fully understood what it felt like to lose a wife - to see her in a coffin; to go to her graveside and bury her. Now I understand."

"And the depth of grief is greater than I could've imagined. The separation is hard. I have hope, an assured hope that I will see her again in heaven. In the meantime there is this lostness – separateness - that in itself is a bit surprising."

As Phyllis was dying she and I talked often about what the experience of heaven would be like. Why is it important for the body to be raised back to life?

Heaven is a mystery.

There's not that much shared about heaven in the Bible other than the fact that God is there.

And now, so is Phyllis.

See you in the morning, Phyl.

CHAPTER 21
Lessons For My Grandchildren

Kaiden, Ryland, Hailey and Hannah are grandchildren who were loved, blessed, interceded for and championed by Phyllis. It was for them this memoir was written.

Information about "Coby," pastoral ministry, and kidney transplants were important for Phyllis to put down on record. However, the following "lessons" for her four grandkids came from deep in her spirit. She shared them just weeks before she passed away.

Lessons For My Grandchildren
1. Bruce and I love you - always and forever. No matter what happens, our love is unconditional and eternal.

2. Real men are kind. Grandkids, you saw Grampa Bruce involved with manly stuff - fixing things with his hands and tools. You also watched Grampa care for me - feed me, wipe my face and be tender with me. Let this be a profound lesson for you to remember about your grandfather and what a real

man does. That's real love.

3. Respect others. Everyone is equal. I was taught at a young age that all races are equal. When I was twelve years old I travelled to New York City with the Endicotts. We went to an NHL game at Madison Square Gardens - the Rangers were playing the Boston Bruins. We went to the Ice Capades and other New York events. I distinctly remember going into a coffee shop in NYC and seeing a sign, "No blacks allowed." It was around New Year's Eve, 1960. The sign really shocked me. I was aware of some American history but to see segregation was shocking.

4. Always tell the truth. I believe that getting away with a lie is the worst thing that can happen to you. It will lead to a deceptive life. Tell the truth.

5. Treat people with dignity. Bruce remembers the first time that Phyllis asked him to feed her. She needed her dignity as much as she needed food.

6. Joy and laughter. Find what makes you smile. I can laugh at myself. There was always laughter in our college dorm. Being with those I care about and love makes me smile. You made me smile.

7. Loyalty to family and friends is so important - maybe the most important thing. Put your family first.

8. Work hard at whatever you do.

9. Apply yourself. Make something of your life.

10. I did not want to be a burden to my mum when I was growing up. In hindsight, I don't think that was the healthiest attitude. Lean on your family.

11. Placing your complete trust in someone else – like in marriage – is challenging. I had to rise to the challenge. I had no outstanding role models of what marriage was like. Whatever challenges you face, rise to them with God's help.

12. Don't focus on the negative. You will miss out so much in life just because you become fixated on the fact that someone may not have spoken to you or you read something very negative into a situation when it's not there at all.

13. Don't carry grudges. No matter how hard I tried, I couldn't carry a grudge. You will miss out in any relational setting - say in a dorm or friendship group - if you do not allow yourself to be vulnerable. Make an attempt to be friendly or fit in and get over past hurts.

14. Bruce took dating seriously. He didn't want to date just to date. He wrote me a letter every day. He made me tear them up. That was the last time I did what I was told. Bruce and I were in the same year of Bible College. Bruce was the Student council President. I was the social convener. We had our picture together and it looked like a wedding picture. When we came into the school cafeteria our classmates clinked glasses like at a wedding reception. When you date, take it seriously.

15. Express your love. Be affectionate. Tell people you love them.

16. Have a keen awareness of danger. I could have been molested when I was seven years old but I was aware of the danger sensation in my body and avoided the situation. The father of a friend was driving her and I to some event. When we arrived he sent his daughter out of the car first. Then he made an advance towards me but did not touch me. I got out of the car before he could touch me.

17. Never talk to strangers.

18. Be still and know that He is God. It may be in your nature, like it was in mine, to want to jump into situations, or try to fix them. My type of personality can get ahead of God in terms of action so being still is a good spiritual discipline. Be reminded that being still allows God to work. In waiting you can hear the voice of God and understand His wisdom for the situation.

Bruce, Shawn and Kris, Robyn,

invite you to join
us in honouring
our wife and mom
at a celebration
with special friends
and family.

October 18, 2004
4:00 pm
Sawmill Restaurant
11560 104 Ave.
Edmonton, AB
(780) 429-2816

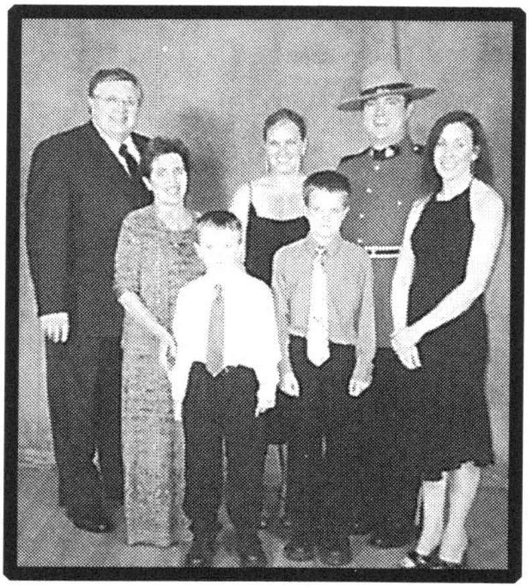

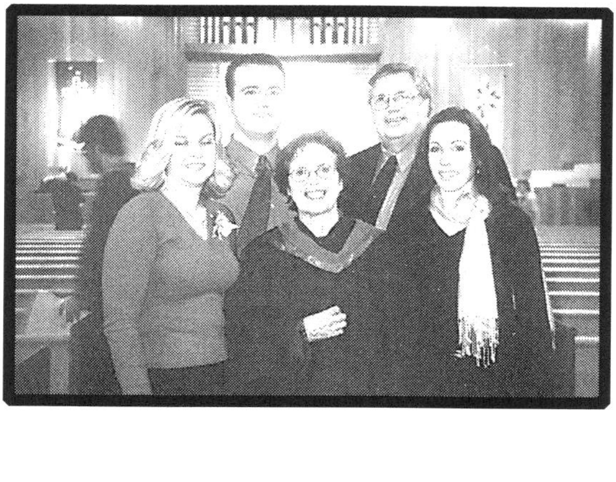

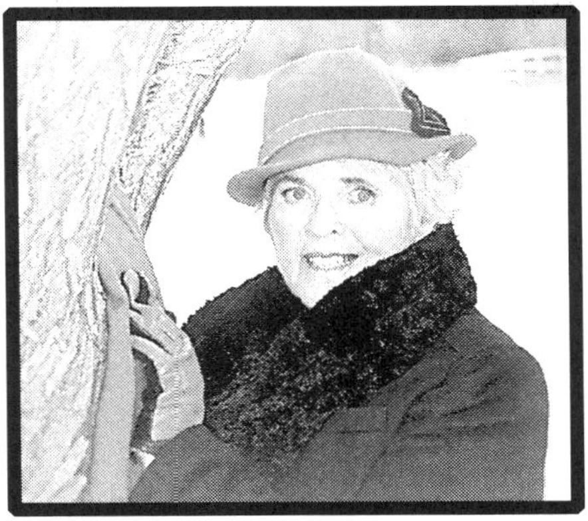

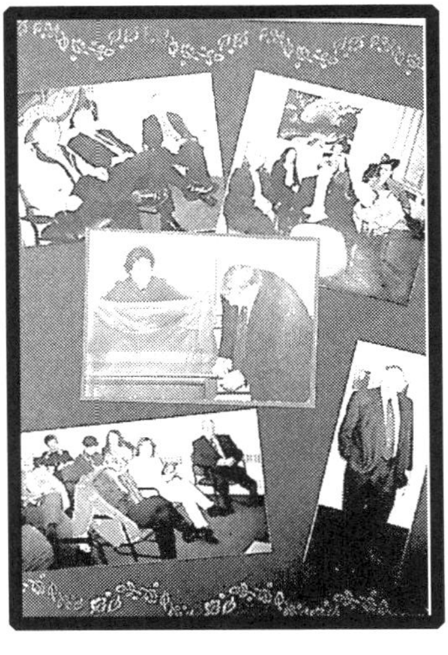

APPENDIX

I	My Girl… By Bruce	117
II	Doubts & Hope	121
III	Memories – Steve & Pattie Hertzog	123
IV	Memories – Ann Harding	127
V	Memories – Marg Gibb	131
VI	Memories – Emmanuel Fonte	135
VII	Bruce's Eulogy	137

APPENDIX I
My Girl... By Bruce

Life for me was changed forever when I noticed a young lady on the Peterborough campus of Eastern Pentecostal Bible college in the fall of 1965. The picture is still vibrant in my mind: confident, big smile, dancing blue eyes and a warm acceptance of anyone she met. Dressed in high heels, white blazer and blue sweater, she captured my attention as she strode the sidewalk toward the C.B. Smith building.

This small-town guy from Vancouver Island, BC was intimidated yet curious, admiring from a distance such a beautiful young lady. I was fortunate that she was in the same class and I found myself keeping an eye on her from my desk toward the back of the class. Sometimes we do things against our better judgement and venture where we have no business venturing.

Such was my audacity when I thought she appeared to be such a wonderful person that I would like to know her as a friend, never thinking it could be anything more. Yet, against my better judgement, this retiring and rather boring fellow began wondering if the impossible was possible. I didn't really care if she had a guy back home, but if she did, he now had some competition. Little did I know at the time that our casual friendship would blossom and eventually flower into us spending the better part of 49 years together.

Shortly after our relationship began, fellow students began tattling to me of her escapades on campus until it became common for me to respond, "what did she do now" as if I bore some responsibility for her. It became a theme of our lives together and I was secretly proud that she was respectful of tradition but not bound by it. Whether in the church or in her secular relationships, she could disarm even the most reserved of traditionalists with her engaging smile and was soon leading her own parades. She was as comfortable with the sinner as she was the saint, often more so.

Her Irish heritage was most important to her and it bequeathed to her a wonderful gift for storytelling. She was one of the most honest people you could know but when reciting incidents of her life she never let the facts get in the way of a good story. We all loved her for it. You may not have noticed, but Phyllis had a mind of her own and usually everyone else came to know what she was thinking. Once, when she and I were having a difference of opinion while living in Kingston, as per usual I was losing the argument, but all I could think was, "I'm really angry with you … but I really love you too". How do you win against that?

Phyllis was a marvelous mother to our children and raised them to become the wonderful individuals they are now. She longed to be with her kids and encourage them in the ways of the Lord.

She was always my rock steady partner in ministry and often was my counsellor when facing what seemed to be heavy responsibilities. She never used her illness to deflect her drive to care for people and it was easy for those looking on to think she never had a care in the world beyond those which they knew about. No husband could be prouder of his partner in life than I have been.

As her life was drawing to a close, her attention turned in a marked way to contemplating eternity. We often chatted about the theology of heaven and the mysteries that escape our ability to understand in time. Her eternal salvation was never in doubt to her, but she agonized over whether Jesus would be pleased with her life on earth when she was to see him.

Increasingly her heart was drawn like a compass needle turning north to seeing the Lord and eventually my girl quietly slipped away to be embraced by her God.

APPENDIX II
Doubts & Hope

"Jesus hears our pleas for help and is patient with our doubts. He does not condemn us. He has paid completely for any sin that is exposed in our pain.

He does not always answer with the speed we desire, nor is his answer always the deliverance we hope for. But he will always send the help that is needed. His grace will always be sufficient for those who trust him. The hope we taste in the promises we trust will often be the sweetest thing we experience in this age. And his reward will be beyond our imagination.

In John's darkness and pain Jesus sent a promise to sustain John's faith. He will do the same for you." Jon Bloom

"Like muscles, hope is made by rising, again and again, lifting the weight of the dark that's conspiring to flatten us with, the strength of His promises that's certain to carry us."

"Hope is not some elusive lottery ticket for the lucky, but hope is the fiery torch the faithful raise in a life-grip to burn back the ugly face of the dark so they can see their promised land — and the welcoming face of God."

"Hope is not the belief that things will turn out well, but the belief God is working through all things, *no matter how things turn out.*"

"And when we get karate kicked in the esophagus by life and it hurts to breathe, we will be the Remembering People who retrace it slow again, how Hope works:

Hope fiercely promises to meet us in hard things now - because we fiercely trust God's promise to make all things new."

"Hope is a defiant reliance on God keeping His Word."

"Hold on to His Word for all you're *worth* — because His Word is what proves God is trustworthy." *Ann Voskamp*

APPENDIX III
Memories – Steve & Patti Hertzog

We are soooo thankful to the Lord for putting Phyllis in our lives. I can honestly say we would never be where we are in ministry today and probably not in ministry at all if it wasn't for the encouragement Phyl & Bruce were to us & the faith she showed in us. (I understand what you saw in Patti, but what you ever saw in this tall skinny Jewish kid from the suburbs... still pretty new in the Lord and with no bible college and no ministry experience whatsoever... is beyond me.)

For all this we owe Phyllis a great debt... which obviously we will never be able to repay.

None the less I would still like to say a HUGE THANK YOU for everything Phyllis poured into our lives and the genuine compassion and love of the Lord she consistently showed us.

Phyllis and Bruce were the absolute best to work in ministry with. They were nicer to us than we deserved (OK, maybe Patti deserved it, but I know I didn't!).

I have seen so many kids who graduated from college go into ministry and then drop out of ministry within a few years because of a negative experience with their senior pastor. Well, a big part of the reason Patti and I are still in ministry today is because when we started out we had such a wonderfully positive experience with our senior pastor (and the rest of the staff too)!

Phyllis always made us feel like we belonged – a part of a team to be sure but perhaps more importantly part of a family. Phyllis had a great knack for that with her humour, her passion for life and ministry, and most of all her genuine care and concern. To this day I have never felt as deep a sense of community or truly as much a part of a team as I did in those early ministry years with you & Bruce, Bob & Denise, Lorne & Maria, Lucie, Norma, etc.

Thanks to you I have absolutely wonderful memories of those years - my formative years in ministry and some of the best years of our lives.

So again, thank you so much Phyllis for being such a great mentor, friend & instructor. I will never forget the lessons you & Bruce taught me: that ministry is a team sport, that men get paid for ministry but "women do it for Jesus," that sometimes in church we need to lighten up & take the bee out of our bonnet (or the pickle out of our bum), and mostly that:

1. People matter more than programs.
2. God is a lot more gracious & forgiving than His people.
3. If you don't get your own way in Church, get over it.
4. Prophetic words should always be tested (I Thessalonians 4:1).
5. When considering people for leadership, look for loyalty and character - almost anything else we can teach them.

Thanks to you, these are lessons I was able to pass on to students at Vanguard for twenty- two years and lessons I am still passing on as I teach in colleges around the world today - to say nothing of everything Phyllis poured into Shawn & Robyn, all the grandkids, Mannie & Nat, Bob & Joc, and so many others. Phyllis' life has produced fruit 30, 60, & 100 times what was sown. She is one amazing lady and although she may not have realized it, this world is an immeasurably better place because God put Phyllis Ryan Fisher in it.

Love you so much.

APPENDIX IV
Memories – Ann Harding

When Rollie and I were married in November 1974, Bruce Fisher had just become our pastor. Phyllis was my first Pastor's wife as a young married woman and was an inspiration to me from the start.

One of the greatest joys of being with Phyllis was her outlook on life and vibrant personality. She loves life and the joy of family and friends. Her laughter is infectious. We took few trips together but one memorable one was to an event in Moncton.

We had another couple with us and their child started asking for a drink about 20 km into an 80 km trip and never stopped until we reached our destination. For months, maybe years, after that when things were quiet, Phyllis would get that gleam in her eye and say "I want a drink" and explode with laughter and of course I would join in.

In spite of her health issues, I cannot ever remember Phyllis being down. She showed the joy of the Lord in her daily life.

She loves the ministry – was devoted to it as much as Bruce was. She often gave a "word" during a testimony service and it was timely, heart felt and meaningful.

She always encourages people to serve the Lord. We did visitation together and I learned so much from her, in her approach to people, her ability to listen to their needs, to sum up their thoughts and bring the conversation back to Christ. Again her sense of humour kept things in balance.

She and I visited in an area of Saint John where in retrospect we probably should not have gone without a male escort! But we did and she was fearless in her dealings with those precious people, many of whom sent their children to Sunday School. We would often knock on a door and see them peeking out from behind a curtain, but they wouldn't answer the door. Phyllis would manage to control the giggle until we were back on the sidewalk…. barely.

Phyllis is transparent and open in her dealings with people. You didn't have to wonder if she agreed with you or not. She could make her point of view very clear but that was something I appreciated about her. There was no animosity in her. You knew exactly what she was thinking.

I remember when she and Bruce were building their home in Saint John. Her cupboard doors weren't on for a long time and she told me that someone had remarked that she had nothing to hide. I remember thinking, "no you don't".

Phyllis is a woman of prayer. She was always in the prayer room before service and always at the altar after service. She encouraged me to also be at the altar and pray for people and helped me grow in this respect.

No matter who you were or when you dropped in to their home, you were always welcome. She often had people in after church and I noticed over the years that she always had something prepared in the fridge for someone after church.

There are other ways that Phyllis influenced my life but I will end with the most recent. When Rollie was killed, she and Bruce picked up the phone and called me. It was a bittersweet moment to hear their voices again but the love and compassion that flowed through that phone was unmistakable.

She is a faithful friend.

APPENDIX V
Memories – Marg Gibb

She was perky and attracted people like bees to honey. There was a natural, pure sweetness to Phyllis Ryan, a young almost 20 year old student who, like all of us, was trying to fit into a college environment.

Homesickness, shyness, and insecurities loomed large on the college campus. Yet, Phyllis shone as a young woman who could create an ease of immediate acceptance by her cuteness, big smile and genuine love for people.

Bruce Fisher, a handsome, talented and full-of-presence guy, was attracted to Phyllis.

He was much more reserved and reflective and needed the outgoing, full-of-life Phyllis at his side.

Together they made that perfect ministry couple that would do well. And they did do well.

Their ministry, over the years, took them from the Maritimes, to Montreal and finally Edmonton, Alberta. Their love for people was evident and it was reciprocated from the young to the old. Their combined wisdom and deep commitment to serve God and fulfill their calling, anchored them in their own development journey.

My personal contact with them included many times when I spoke at various gatherings while they pastored in Evangel, Montreal, and a special week of teaching on prayer at Central Tabernacle in Edmonton, Alberta. Later it became 2-3 phone calls per year to "check-in" and "catch-up". These were long conversations covering our current life-happenings, memories of the past and always meaningful discussions on what we were experiencing and learning in ministry and leadership development.

Our conversations revealed the heart and strength of Phyllis Fisher. Her kidney transplant years ago, was only one of the huge obstacles she overcame. Bruce and Phyllis, like most leaders, had to face the enormous challenges of leadership and make the choice to grow. Later in life, health challenges brought changes they never anticipated. But Phyllis was not a quitter!

Beneath the surface of her charming ways was a woman who was tenacious and deeply anchored in her relationship with Jesus. Her identity never came from her role, or her position, or the circumstances she found herself in. Her identity came from her rock-solid faith.

After a necessary move to Ponoka, Alberta, Phyllis dug in to become more. Defeat was not in her vocabulary. Her work as a Chaplain at the Centennial Centre for Mental Health stretched her as a person, minister and leader. How would her faith work out in a non-church environment - a world she'd lived in and functioned well in for many years? Here her world was so very different - a world of professionals in mental health, broken families and often difficult-to-relate-to patients. Yet she won their hearts and their trust.

Phyllis as Chaplain developed deeper in grace and mercy. My conversations with her during this time revealed her openness to see God at work in new ways - not seen in her church environments. Her insights were refreshing!

When cancer struck her body, once again Phyllis' spirit remained like always- strong. She had the ability to even make light of the cancerous tumours on her hands and face. Her zest for life would not be diminished. Her beauty shone through. Doctors marveled at her tenacity and the repeated miracles.

She messaged me one day to tell me she was coming to Ontario to see friends. Because of my overseas work, I was not able to join the many get-togethers planned for Phyllis. At the time, I didn't realize the importance of her desire to be with her friends. She was saying goodbye.

My last conversation with Phyllis was April 18, 2017. She called from palliative care. Her voice was weak but that same spunk was there. No despair but hope! Hope in resurrection power. Hope in seeing her friends and family again, one day. Hope in her eternal relationship with Jesus, the One she loved and served...with her whole heart.

It has been said: *"Some people come into our lives and quickly go. Some stay for a while and leave footprints on our hearts, and we are never the same again."*

Phyllis was that kind of friend. I will never be the same again.

Margaret Gibb
Founder & Director
Women Together
women-together.org

APPENDIX VI
Memories – Emmanuel Fonte

I first met Phyllis in 1983 when she and Pastor Bruce came to Montreal to lead my home church Evangel.

At the time, I was very involved in the music program, conducting the orchestra and other music groups. It was obvious with one look at me that music was the only thing keeping me going back there. Phyllis recognized that immediately.

At the time, my life wasn't conforming to the standards that would be expected of someone on a church stage. Rather than request my resignation, Bruce was supportive and pastoral. Often, Phyl would touch my shoulder. That touch that says 'you are loved', 'you are welcome here'. On a particular Sunday evening, when the altar call came, as she walked forward to pray with those at the front, she put her hand on my back and guided me from my seat to the prayer benches that lined the altar area of Evangel. Manipulative? Possibly. Done out of love? Absolutely!

In 1989, while I was in Edmonton interviewing for the position of music director for what was at the time Central Tabernacle (later to become North Pointe), a board representative from that church was observing Bruce, Phyllis' husband back in Montreal. I chose to take the position in Montreal that fall. That New Year's Eve, at Bruce's bedside in Montreal, Nathalie and I accepted his invitation to move out west to serve with them in Edmonton at Central Tabernacle. Leaving home, and all we had ever known was easier because we would be with Phyl and Bruce. Our time with them in Edmonton is some of the most cherished memories we have. She loved us well in our partnership of ministry.

Phyl and I share the same birthday so I never forgot to sing to her, no matter where we are geographically. Occasionally, she was a second mother to me. There were a few times that she entrusted her two kids to Nathalie and me. We walked many challenging adventures with Shawn and Robin. Looking back, we were all kids, and didn't know anything. Phyl was always encouraging and loving. And the laugh! When she laughs, it is contagious.

When I think of all I've learned from Phyl, the characteristic that stands out to me is mercy. While she and I may have debated theology, and often saw the church rules differently, she demonstrated kindness and compassion for everyone. She taught me to see the humanity in others. She exemplifies what it means to be Jesus on this earth.

Phyllis Fisher is the light of the world!

APPENDIX VII
Bruce's Eulogy

Sixty-nine years ago, Phyllis Ryan Fisher was born in Toronto to a loving and resourceful mother who in post war years either cared directly for Phyllis or made sure she was nurtured in wonderful homes surrounded by people who "adopted" her into their families.

Although Phyllis was an only child she collected moms and dads and sisters along the way that enriched her life and helped mold her into the lady she grew to be. This small-town girl loved the water and the Kawartha Lake country where she grew up and never forgot the friends who all loved her as a local girl who was going to make her mark in life.

During three wonderful years in Bible College she made friends that have cared about and reached out to Phyllis for the rest of her life. The tributes expressed recently via social media are testament to the way she could welcome people into her life and love them as family.

Phyllis was struck with serious illness soon after college and met the challenge of committing her vows to Bruce Fisher by asking to be released from hospital the night before her wedding and then returning to a rigorous schedule of kidney dialysis after a couple of days honeymooning in Niagara Falls in October of 1968.

Phyllis eventually received a kidney from an unknown donor, whose family in their grief from losing a daughter in a fatal Toronto car accident, contributed the gift of life to a critically ill, unknown recipient. They probably do not know that their gift kept our Phyllis alive and in excellent renal health for over thirty years.

From these challenging days just to stay alive, Phyllis was to begin a journey that defied the best predictions of her dedicated doctors. They suggested that she would never be far away from the health support of the medical community in Toronto, never be a mother, probably not live for many years as transplantation was a relatively new development in medical science, and certainly not take on the responsibilities of a career.

In hindsight, we can now detail that Phyllis was not only able to be released from her caring medical community in Toronto, she ended up moving to Kingston, Ontario, Lyttleton, Saint John and Moncton, all in New Brunswick, Montreal, Quebec and then to Edmonton, Alberta.

She shared her love with wonderful congregations of these towns and cities and gained innumerable friends along the way. During these years she accepted and functioned at a high level as a pastor's wife, encourager-in-chief to many young people, led bible studies, taught Sunday School, counseled those whose trust she accepted and cherished.

Phyllis went on to be a preacher in her own right and was recognized by her denomination by being ordained. Phyllis also moved to and lived in Sylvan Lake and Ponoka during her tenure as a chaplain.

In 1972 Phyllis became mother to her son Shawn. Her gifts as a mom were evident immediately and she couldn't wait to receive her daughter, Robyn in 1975. Phyllis took hold of her home and welded four unrelated-by-blood members into the loving family that she presided over to her death.

With equal enthusiasm, she embraced the arrival of grandsons Kaiden and Ryland, then later, Hailey and Hannah. Who could have ever known that this family would come into being and be glued together by the love and encouragement of this extraordinary lady besought by illness most of her life.

When Bruce was sidelined by illness for many years, Phyllis just got on with life and fashioned a career in Chaplaincy that saw her associate with wonderful supervisors and fellow students and then go on be a practical guide and encourager to so many in health institutions and prison facilities.

While balancing a home and career and addressing medical challenges, Phyllis pursed and obtained a Master's Degrees in her field.

It was during this time that Phyllis developed a circle of professional friends with whom she stayed closely in touch for the rest of her life, Caroline, Lynn and Lorna, self-titled the "Sunshine Ladies".

It was also during this time that another fellow professional, Karen McLeod, extended to Phyllis the gift of life by becoming a living donor and giving one of her own kidneys after Phyllis's original kidney failed. The Fishers will be forever grateful to Karen.

Phyllis will always be remembered for her zest for life and the wonderful contributions she made to so many people over the years.

Phyllis was wife, mother, mother-in-law and grandmother extraordinaire.

She is missed so much.

ACKNOWLEDGEMENTS

This memoir was crafted with a generous dose of TLC. Thank you to: Shareen Baker of CREATIVIMPACT for the cover design and photos; Cyana Gaffney of BLUE SKY PUBLISHING for formatting my content and making it publication ready; each one who contributed stories, memories and tributes about Phyllis; Bruce for your decades long mentorship and sharing your memories of Phyllis.

ABOUT THE AUTHOR

Rev. Bob Jones has been a PAOC pastor since 1980; currently he serves as Lead Pastor at North Pointe Community Church, in Edmonton, Alberta. Bob is a recovering perfectionist, who collects Coca-Cola memorabilia and drinks Iced Tea. His office walls are adorned with his sons' framed football jerseys, and his library shelves, with soul food. Married to Jocelyn, father and grandfather. Author of "Ornament: The Faith, Hope and Joy of Kristen Fersovitch" available online at Chapters.ca or Amazon.ca

Follow his blog at http://blog.northpointechurch.ca/ and on Twitter @bobjones49ers

Made in the USA
Lexington, KY
02 July 2018